DO IT
Anyway
GIRL

A Playful, Simple, Unique Guide to Achieving Success in Network Marketing

MICHELLE CUNNINGHAM

Do It Anyway, Girl

A Playful, Simple, Unique Guide to Achieving Success in Network Marketing

Michelle Cunningham
30628 Detroit Road #221
Westlake, OH 44145 USA

MichelleCunningham.com

For permission requests, speaking inquiries, and bulk order purchase options, email support@michellecunninghamonline.com.

ISBN: 978-1-7361058-0-1

Interior Design by Transcendent Publishing
Cover Design by Ryan Biore
Front Cover Photo by Shannon Ahlstrand
Back Cover Photo by Johnathan R. Andujar
Editing by Lori Lynn Enterprises

Printed in the United States of America

Dedication

This book is dedicated to my mom, Paulette. A woman who had so little, defied odds, and created her own dream life. Mom, you inspire me, and I love you. Thank you for always being my rock and for believing in me.

Contents

Praise

There are lots of books on the market for network marketers, but this one comes from a very unique perspective. Michelle grew up with limited resources, was an introvert most of her life, and struggled for the first six years in network marketing. Evidence that if you just never quit and you give it all you've got, success will find its way to you. Must read!

  —**Ray Higdon**, International Bestselling Author, *Freakishly Effective Social Media for Network Marketing*

We need more people like Michelle! This book is perfect for those wanting to finally break through and make things happen with their Network Marketing Business! Coming from an introvert, this speaks so clearly to me! Get your copy, you won't regret it.

  —**Frazer Brookes,** International Bestselling Author, *I Dare You* and *I Double Dare You*

Right from the first chapter, you will feel Michelle's heart and know that this book is not a bunch of fluff & hype. She has an incredible ability to make you come to a dead stop, reflect on your life, hold up a mirror, deal with it, and have a breakthrough all in 5 minutes! Her style of writing is so simple for the reader to grasp and her raw authentic teachings will inspire you to step out and into who you were made to really become. I can't wait to have my team dive into it!

  —**Sarah Zolecki**, Multi-Million Dollar Earner, Network Marketing

Michelle Cunningham is directly responsible for my business exploding because of her simple and duplicatable systems. She has learned all the things for network marketing that work as well as what doesn't work. She takes all of her knowledge and presents it in a simple manner to help everyone succeed instead of having to make the same mistakes she has. Michelle gives you a blueprint of how to succeed faster, more efficiently, and more abundantly. I owe her a huge acknowledgment for completely transforming my business.

—**Stephanie Blake**, Top 1% Network Marketer

If you're looking for a great play-by-play approach to grow your network marketing business, then *Do It Anyway, Girl* is it. Michelle lays out all the groundwork for you on how to approach your prospects, your business, and your team members. All you have to do is apply it. It's basically fail-proof.

—**Julie Burke**, Network Marketing Leader
& Online Business Mentor

This book would have changed my business when I first got started in Network Marketing! I wish I had had it ten years ago! I know I wouldn't have struggled as much as I did. What I can say about Michelle is she's just a REAL coach with REAL strategies that actually work to build a successful network marketing business. This book truly gives a detailed breakdown of the action steps she took to build an insane business on social media. As an introvert myself, it was such a breath of fresh air to know I am not alone. Introverts can recruit too, and she breaks it down in this incredible book! This is a total must-read!

—**Marina Simone**, President of Moms & Heels | 7-Figure Earner | Expert Online Course Launcher & Online Coach

Michelle is simply masterful! She's the girl next door who has seemingly figured it all out and is happy to share the goods. This book not only gives you the blueprint to be able to create success in your NWM business (scripts and all), but it also stretches you to think BIG! I smiled the entire time I was reading this book, and my heart was filled with joy. This book left me truly INSPIRED!

—**Charyse Williams**, RN, Holistic Empowerment Coach

I literally just finished reading the whole thing, and all I can say is "WOW!!!" I'm going to buy hundreds of copies and give them to my team as gifts because there is such wisdom with incredible training. It has everything they need to be successful!!

—**Maggie Rader**, Top 1% Network Marketing Leader

When I found Michelle Cunningham on YouTube®, it felt like I was her long lost bestie. She is down to earth, funny, smart, and sincere. She treats you like you are important and really invests in your success. Her knowledge of business and creating valuable content are worth their weight in gold. She will expand your vision and get you out of your comfort zone. Reading this book, you will realize you can do anything because she proves it.

—**Sonia Molina**, Top 1% Network Marketing Leader | Entrepreneur | Coach | John Maxwell Mindset Coach

This book was a true beacon of light and has pushed me to level up, dream bigger, and own my awesome! It's a true, undeniable blueprint to navigating our industry and packed with tons of behind the scenes insights.

—**Shamecca Stephens**, The "How-To Entrepreneur"

If you struggle with booking and recruiting, this book is for you! It gave me play-by-play strategies on how to recruit and book for my direct sales business. Michelle shares exactly what she said and did to become successful. She keeps it light and simple! I highly recommend this book for anyone who wants to up-level their life and direct sales business.

—**Dorothy-Inez Del Tufo**, Confidence Coach

Can I just say, "WOW!" Michelle is honest, relatable, and hilarious! Her principles are duplicatable, you know exactly what to do, and by the end of the book, you feel completely inspired to DO IT ANYWAY, GIRL!

—**Noukouchee Xiong**, Independent Consultant,
Network Marketing

For those struggling in their Direct Sales business or looking to leverage their social media game more efficiently, Michelle has the perfect solution in this entertaining yet practical guide. I was laughing throughout the book, but I was totally sucked in! I found I couldn't put it down! I believe everyone building a business needs to read this book!

—**Kimberly Olson**, Bestselling Author | Top Recruiter |
Podcaster | Coach & Creator of The Goal Digger Girl

Michelle inspires and motivates with her whole heart! Her super simple, yet ridiculously effective methods, were a game-changer for my direct sales business. Within six months of implementing her techniques, I was promoted to the top 1% of my company and quadrupled not only my team size but also my income. If you want to have massive growth in your business, and you want it simple and fast, then get this book!

—**Sierra Tippens**, Top 1% Network Marketing Leader

If you're looking for a book that will teach you how to step up your game and help you reach the top of your company, this is the book! It's jam-packed full of tips, strategies, and scripts you can use today! Girl, you need to just buy the book! I'm a personal development junkie and it's one of the best I've read!

—**Stacey Killam**, Network Marketing Leader

FOREWORD

*M*ichelle is a girl who defied all odds in life, her career, and business—and decided to "do it anyway" and at times "do it afraid!" Her rise to the top (after failing forward a few years) is an encouragement to anyone who has started their business—and perhaps restarted—with the courage and will to succeed. After all, in this business, your "willing to" must be greater than your "wanting to."

Are you willing to do WIT? *Whatever It Takes?* If so, this book is for you! *Do it Anyway, Girl* is like a business BFF for direct sales—leveraging real-life stories and experiences in a relatable way. The author shares her struggles and how she found solutions each step of the way.

This practical guide is exactly what you need when learning how to talk to new people, set up presentations, share your business, conquer the most common objections, get those digits, and keep your leads funnel full.

Will your journey be easy? No. But it will be worth it.

Your journey in direct sales is worth it. It allows you to choose a dream life, versus a dream job. All while presenting fabulous opportunities for personal and professional growth. And it doesn't just pay well—you get recognized well. Not to mention the fun, friendships, and fabulous opportunities for personal and professional growth along the way.

Take this journey with Michelle, step by step. Put into action the steps and scripts she gives you. Be encouraged by the stories—and HER story! And think about what success in network marketing will mean to YOUR story ... Your "why" is worth it. There is nothing like seeing *your* reason why in action!

So let's do this!

Be a student of this business. Read this book again and again. Gift one to each new team member as a getting-started guide. The more who "know," the more your team will grow!

Rock on, rock star! You've got this!

—**Sarah Robbins**, Bestselling Author of *ROCK Your Network Marketing Business*

Chapter One

Discovering
"The Best Thing EVER!"

"You should try to get a job as a pharmaceutical rep," my friend says. "It's super lucrative."

We were just broke college students at the time, but I'll never forget when Mark (my super-smart friend who is now a surgeon) told me this because he followed it up with, "Actually, it's nearly impossible to land a job as a pharmaceutical sales rep right out of college. Never mind."

Even though I'm not the least bit interested in anything related to medicine, I decide this is the job I have to have. I take his statement as a challenge. And I want to prove him wrong.

I go on Google and find a book about how to land a job as a pharmaceutical sales rep. I study it over and over and then apply everything in the book.

The book tells me to call all the local pharmaceutical sales reps and tell them I am a college student looking to get into the industry and I want to learn more and shadow them.

This is totally out of my comfort zone, but the book makes me do it. So I do it.

I study the industry, the company, and the competition. I learn it all.

I also have one very strict rule for my party-animal roommates: "If the phone rings in the dorm, no matter when the call comes in, tell whomever it is that I am out for a run."

(This was before cell phones were a thing.)

For my interview, they fly me all the way from Ohio to Boston, and I nail it.

They can't believe a college student would shadow other pharmaceutical reps and decide this was the job she had to have. They are impressed.

But, they want to test me. So, the next week, they call me at 7 a.m. on a Saturday.

Now, 7 a.m. on a Saturday meant I had been drinking the night before (after my shift at Applebee's™) and was now at my boyfriend's dorm still sleeping.

But my roommate answers the call and informs the nice man— my future boss—that I am out for a run.

That seals the deal. I land the job.

He later tells me that he is so impressed a college student would be out for a run at 7 a.m. on a Saturday that he knows I must be a go-getter.

I later tell him the truth, but by that point, I am already in.

About six months into my new pharmaceutical sales gig in Massachusetts, driving my new free company car, enjoying my shiny new laptop, and managing an expense account of over $20,000 to spend on doctors' offices to bring them food and treats, I decide …

I am bored.

Wake up.

Throw on business suit and makeup.

Get in car.

Drive around.

Smile.

Talk to doctors for 30 seconds.

Go home.

Workout.

Go to bed.

Wake up.

Do it again.

I feel like, *Is this really all there is to life?*

I am missing the race. I was used to working so hard my whole life, and the harder I worked, the more money I made. But now, when I am making a salary, I see that race being taken away from me.

The more I work, the *same* I make.

If I work harder than those around me, my paycheck doesn't change. The challenge is gone.

It makes me feel empty. *If you've ever felt that way, you are a bonafide entrepreneur stuck in a job that you need to rise out of.*

Then ... the MAGIC OPPORTUNITY presents itself.

My coworker tells me that his wife has a full-time job but also has a little side-gig selling products for a home party company.

He asks me if I want to go to a hotel event with her to see more.

As a single girl with nothing going on, I agree because, well, I had nothing going on.

I walk into the Holiday Inn® that evening, enter a ballroom, and see about 30 women who are all smiling and hugging.

One lady in the room claims to make 6-figures working from home.

Another is there to celebrate earning her free company car.

And another claims she has earned millions in her career.

At 23 years old, I am sitting there with my mind blown.

I look around that room in bewilderment thinking that this sounds like the best opportunity in the world.

Work from home, make unlimited income, no boss, free cars, millions of dollars ... Like WHO WOULDN'T want to do this?

I am so excited that I leave that meeting ready to quit my job and join the company.

I call my mom to let her know that I just learned about this amazing opportunity that allows me to work from home and make money with no boss, and I am going to become a millionaire.

I hear a long pause on the other end of the line.

A long, awkward pause.

She breaks the silence with: "Oh, honey. Being successful in network marketing is really hard."

I listen, hang up the phone, and sleep on it.

Then, I think about it for a full week before I accept that I am 23.

At 23, I don't have to listen to my mom anymore.

I love my mom.

I respect my mom.

But I also don't want my mom's job.

We are different.

She likes to sit at a computer all day.

I don't.

I like movement.

I like a challenge.

I like the race.

For my entire life, the harder I worked, the more money I made. As an hourly employee, if I worked more hours, I made more money. As a salaried employee in pharmaceutical sales, I was expected to work and work and make the same pay each week. Boring and deflating for someone who likes the race.

I figure I'll try my luck at this home-based business alongside my current job.

I meet the leader at a Friendly's™ restaurant, hear her inspiring story of success, and I am even giddier than before. I am ALL in.

So much so, that I whip out my credit card and invest $3,000 in inventory to start my business.

I go home that night on a cloud. I can't stop thinking about this opportunity. Nor can I stop thinking about how perfect it is for everyone in the world. *Literally everyone.*

I actually can't imagine anyone doing anything other than this once they hear about it. That's how amazing this opportunity is in my crazy newbie eyes.

I even think, *I can't imagine why people would want to work for the company fulfilling orders in the shipping department when they could be out selling with this amazing opportunity.*

Needless to say, I had found my thing.

It gave me hope and made my heart come alive.

I was ready to change the world.

Little did I know the world was about to change *me.*

Chapter Two

Who Is Michelle Cunningham?

That was back in 2002. It's now 2020, and not only have I become a top 1% leader of a network marketing business, but I am also the founder of a 7-figure online brand. My name is Michelle Cunningham, and I come from some pretty humble beginnings.

I grew up in a small Connecticut town called East Granby, population 4,500.

There was one stoplight in the center of town near the fire department. To get to any store, you'd have to drive at least twenty minutes.

In this little New England town, everyone knew everyone. The good, the bad, the ugly. Everyone knew everything *about* everyone, too.

In that little town where everyone knew everyone, my family was "the different family." You see, my parents married, had three kids, and then divorced.

When my mother became the sole caregiver for us, my brother was seven, I was six, and my younger brother was three.

My mom did whatever she could to make money. She opened a daycare in our home so she could be with us and afford the bills. At night, she cleaned houses.

Most of the time she provided enough money to just get by, but sometimes something big would break in the house (like the water heater), and then we were poor for months and months.

It was in those times that I realized we were different than the middle-class kids around us. We would get in our car, drive to the church, and go to the basement. They had special shelves stocked with extra canned foods and boxed foods like ramen noodles that we could go pick up when our shelves were bare.

My brothers and I thought it was fun to go to the church after hours when no one was around to fill up bags with food. It felt like such a treat.

But I realized when we were driving home, watching my mom with tears streaming down her face and hearing her sniffles, that this wasn't the life she wanted for us.

She wanted more. We just didn't have more.

In those years, when we were broke, and Christmas would come around, we knew it was going to be "one of those" Christmases.

Those were the Christmases when every gift under the tree was in a different wrapping paper color and labeled "Boy Age 7," "Girl Age 6," or "Boy Age 3."

We knew those were the years that my mom couldn't afford gifts, and it was our community that had come together to help this poor little family in town.

While I was always thankful for the community members that came together to love on us, I also felt a sadness associated with it. It felt like we were that poor little family that needed hand-outs. I didn't want to be that family. It felt empty to need to have others take care of us. And every time I played with those toys, it was a reminder of what we couldn't afford.

The fierce little person inside of me at that age knew that I wanted to be on the other end of that giving. I wanted to be the family giving to others. I wanted to have abundance. I wanted to help others.

But, the reality was, we didn't have anything more to give monetarily.

We were different.

How different we were always became wildly evident when I visited my friends' homes who had real Christmas with real, legit gifts. Real board games, lotions and perfumes, electronic games, cars with remotes, books galore, and clothes. They didn't just get a gift. They got GIFTS. Lots of them.

But, I'll tell you what. My mom had two very special gifts.

Gift 1: She was creative.

At Easter, the Easter Bunny always ran out of his budget by the time he got to our house, so instead, our Easter Bunny would bring peanuts and hide hundreds throughout the house.

If you found the peanut with a smiley face on it, you would get a special egg with chocolate.

And, my mom would celebrate that smiley peanut like it was the best thing since sliced bread.

Gift 2: She was loving.

She was a frequent giver of hugs, kisses, and quality time. It was all she could afford. Love.

She knew how to make us feel important.

That's a big gift and a big lesson. Love is free.

So, I grew up feeling loved.

My loving heart hated seeing my mom struggle. I watched her struggle to get money out of the ATM and put groceries back that we couldn't afford. I also watched her cry quietly because raising three kids with very little money was hard. It was exhausting. It felt helpless. I could sense that.

As a six-year-old, I knew one thing. I wanted to have money when I got older. I knew that money equated to choices. Choices we didn't have.

My friends around me could afford stuff.

All kinds of stuff.

Like Pantene® shampoo.

And BIG crisp apples.

And new outfits on the first day of school.

And new cleats for soccer.

I vividly remember standing at CVS Pharmacy®, staring at Pantene shampoo and conditioner, and dreaming of the day we would be able to afford THAT shampoo. That's what the rich kids used.

We used whichever 79¢ shampoo-plus-conditioner was on sale.

I dreamt of the day that I would use Pantene.

My friend Kristin always had fresh apples at her house—not the ones in the bag—the ones you actually hand-select and put in a bag. You know, the rich people apples. The EXPENSIVE ONES.

We had Little Debbie™ snacks because they were 10 for 99¢. Unhealthy food is cheaper.

I never got a new outfit on the first day of school. I never really asked for one, even though I knew that was important to fit in. We couldn't afford new ones, and I didn't want to put pressure on my mom.

I'll never forget standing on the soccer field in 10th grade wearing my Kmart™ cleats that were ripped across the top and down the side where the laces were. We just couldn't afford new ones. We were playing an opposing team, and they were from the "really rich" town next door.

This little chick standing next to me on the soccer field with her $200 brand-name cleats, all shiny, laced beautifully, looked down at my cleats and said, "Nice cleats. Tell your parents to buy you some new cleats. You're a mess."

Back then, my response was silence. My inward response was sadness. First, I had a single mom. Second, we didn't have money.

Either way, I came from nothing and always felt less than those around me. And people like Mean Cleat Chick didn't help.

So, I retreated inward. Hiding and being quiet was a bit easier than trying to stand out in middle and high school.

In middle school, I realized that if I wanted to have things, it was going to be up to me. I had the power to work hard to earn money.

So ... I started a babysitting business as a 13-year-old and babysat just about every day for special needs kids. I love kids. Always have. They just make my heart dance with the cute things they discover and say.

I also mowed lawns for $25 a pop at 15 years old. I was a skinny little thing with string bean arms, and I wasn't strong enough to stop the lawnmower before it slammed into the back of people's homes. I would leave these rubbery, black scuff marks all up and down the sides of their homes. It was my trademark.

The Michelle Black Scuff House Special.

Come to think of it, no one ever complained about my trademark. Or if they did, I have a pretty good "bad" memory. I erase bad memories. Except Mean Cleat Chick.

When I turned 16, I was so excited. I could finally WORK a real job.

So, I worked two jobs. One was Dunkin'® Donuts and the other was a candy shop in the center of the mall in one of those kiosks. I picked places to work that people were happy to visit.

I ate Boston cream donuts, buttered popcorn jelly beans, and Sour Patch Kids™ all throughout high school.

I had the metabolism of a hummingbird, so I could eat anything and not gain weight.

Random fact: Hummingbirds have the fastest metabolism of any animal on earth.

No, I'm not an animal expert. But, I am an expert at something called Googling. I believe we can figure everything out with Google™.

So, these two fun jobs helped pay for all the things I needed in high school and allowed me to eat unlimited junk while saving for college. Junk food and money. A dream come true in high school.

Those two jobs allowed me to earn money to buy things to fit in, and I saved what was left over in a bank account to pay for college.

I got accepted into a small college in Ohio called Marietta College. I lived on campus and had a blast.

But, I had to pay for college on my own.

I worked nearly 40 hours from Friday–Sunday at Applebee's while living on campus. Every Friday at about 4 p.m., I would walk through the dorms with my apron on and my Applebee's polo shirt tucked into my khaki pants on my way to work.

Just about everyone I walked by, cracking open their first beer of the night, would say, "That sucks. Have fun at work."

That was my reality. I didn't have money, so I had to earn it. Those kids had money somehow.

But, I didn't really mind my gig. I kind of loved working there.

It helped me get out of my shell. It forced me to talk to people and made me more social.

I consider it one of the best self-growth jobs I ever took because as an introvert, it was really hard to have to talk to strangers. The worst was when one of my customer's food was missing or late, I'd have to tell the cooks in the back. But it was so loud back there, the only way I could get my message across was to yell seriously loud.

So, I started to yell for the things I needed. The alternative was that my customer was going to yell at me and that was actually ten times worse.

But, this yelling helped me realize my power. When I'd carry that plate of hot food out to a customer, I'd feel so accomplished that my voice had actually made something happen.

I learned the faster I worked and the more I connected with people, the more money I made in tips. And that paid for college. I forced myself to talk it up. I got to know people and built friendships.

I would get home from work late, around 11 p.m. or 12 a.m., and by that point, every college student was hammered—like, really hammered.

I always joined in when things were just getting interesting.

It was funny. Oh, the stories I can tell of drunk college kids. Maybe that's another book? It certainly wouldn't work in this one.

Okay, maybe just one. It's one of the few appropriate ones I can share. It's just this one moment I'll never forget … The college guys had a milk-drinking contest. There were about ten of them. We were hooting and hollering from our dorm windows looking down at them. They were ferociously drinking gallons of milk and throwing up all over the front lawn of my dorm. Really. It was gross. At first, it was funny, and then it was just gross and weird.

Anyway, I was still pretty broke all through college. All my money went to tuition.

I had no car because I couldn't afford that—I borrowed my roommate's car a lot so I could get to work. I didn't rush a sorority because you had to have money for that—that was for the rich kids. I rotated lots of the same outfits at college and borrowed clothes to look cute—anything to try to fit in with the kids with money.

While others got handouts, I learned very early on that if I wanted something, I had to work for it.

Hard work gave me the ability to make money so I could fit in and be normal.

That's the first lesson I discovered as an entrepreneur: If it's to be, it's up to me.

Today, as the creator of MichelleCunningham.com, I empower women to rock their direct sales business so they can live more freely, give more generously, and be completely present for the ones they love.

Now, the good news is that I'm not some super wizard who signed up for network marketing and shot immediately to the top.

Those success stories can make you think something is wrong with you.

Actually, I was terrible for six full years before I caught a break.

Yes, SIX YEARS of terribleness.

Then, I made a change and everything shifted. That shift is what this book is about.

Join me as I take you on the journey from zero to laptop-lifestyle income with some laughable stories and lessons learned.

Most importantly, I will share with you the strategies I used, the scripts I followed, and the daily agenda I implemented to grow my failed business into a powerhouse organization.

That journey will take you through how I grew my business by meeting strangers locally, to sending text messages, to using social media, and how I used the power of video to exponentially grow my business.

I have built *all the ways* so you'll learn lots of various strategies in this book that you can apply to your business.

The best part? I'm just a shy girl from humble beginnings.

Growing up, I didn't believe I had any gifts or special powers.

I certainly didn't think I'd amount to anything other than a 9-to-5 employee checking the box.

If you have limiting beliefs, I get it. I did, too—for most of my life.

In this book, I'm not going to talk endlessly about mindset and tell you that you can do it. While I do believe that, I failed for six years while others told me I could do it.

Ultimately, I failed because I needed to change my thoughts.

Then, I needed a guide book.

I needed the next step.

I needed an action plan.

I needed magic scripts.

I needed direction.

So, that's what you'll get from me.

Simple, actionable steps with real-life stories of how to get unstuck, step into your magnificence, make some money, and lead others to success.

Ultimately, change your life for the better.

Money isn't everything, but with money comes choices. Choices to live the life of your dreams.

Chapter Three

Dreaming Is Easy, Doing Is Hard

When I first get started in network marketing back in 2002, I decide to go ALL in with my business.

Wanting to model her success, I ask my leader what to do next.

She tells me that I have to start by first selling to my friends and family.

Now, remember, the year is 2002. There is no text messaging, and there is no Facebook™ at this point.

Ironically, I have just moved to a new town, have one local friend, and all my family lives hours away.

"What now?" I ask.

She then recommends that I start chatting with ladies out and about in parking lots and at grocery stores. She says to just approach them, smile, compliment them, and start a conversation.

Now, being the introvert that I am, I can't imagine a more horrifying situation, but I am ready for this. After all, I've found my thing.

I boldly tell her that tomorrow I will start doing that all day and make this thing work.

While I'm out selling pharmaceuticals and talking to people, I have my business cards in my pocket, so I am going to bring this up to my doctor's office staff friends that I meet along the way.

I will just casually bring it up.

First office. Before I walk in, I practice what I will say in the car. I walk in. I have my business cards ready. Then, I totally freeze. I can't bring up my secret new business.

Second office. I feel regretful, so this time I am going to do it. No questions asked. I will tell someone I now sell for this company. And I chicken out.

Third office. Feeling deflated at this point with my lack of courage, I convince myself that I am going to tell the ladies in the office that I now sell this product and they should host a party, but I have no clue how to say it. So I say nothing.

Fourth office. I give up. *What is wrong with me?*

Fifth office. I leave my business cards in the car and decide to stop killing myself over this. I'm not bringing it up. *Maybe this feeling means it's not meant to be.*

But, I have $3,000 of inventory in my closet at home. What am I going to do?

Later that week, I am at a bank.

In this moment of courage, I see a nice lady filling out her bank deposit slip. I decide THIS is the perfect moment to approach my first human about my business.

Can you imagine a more awkward time than when someone is jotting down their private bank information on a sheet?

But, I push that aside and approach her in the middle island of the bank anyway.

"Hi, sorry, but you are so pretty, and I just love your makeup … and I just started selling for a new company … and I, ummm, I wondered … if you'd like to try our products?"

I don't even know what I'm saying. I'm just saying something, which makes me feel powerful for a second.

She smiles and says, "Oh, that would be nice."

I'm thinking, *This is a walk in the park … I'm so good at this.*

I say, "Great, what's your phone number? I'll call you!"

And she gives it to me. I jot it down on a little piece of receipt I pull out of my purse that was crumbled up with a big wad of gum stuck in it.

Professionalism to the core.

I walk away crowing like the winner I am.

I call my leader to tell her I got A NUMBER. Yes, I GOT A NUMBER.

She seems mildly unimpressed that I only have one, but I know what it took to get one number. She informs me I need to call the woman.

Ugh. Okay. Call her. Yikes.

I wait a few days, building up courage, and I finally call. She doesn't answer. I leave a message. It's messy. "Hi, Veronica. Great to meet you at the, ummm, bank. I know you wanted to try our, ummm, products so let's book a time. Call me. Michelle."

I forget to leave my number.

But I'm too scared to call back, so I wait two days.

Two days later, I call back and say, "Hi, Veronica. It's Michelle from [Company Name]. I forgot to leave you my number when I called, but here it is: [xxx-xxx-xxxx]. Call me soon, and we can get together. I can even bring my goodies to you."

And now, I know she has my number, so it's only a matter of minutes before she'll call back.

But guess what? She doesn't.

She must be on vacation. Or maybe in the hospital. Or maybe she is too shy to call me. Or maybe she's not getting the message because her machine is deleting them. Or maybe she's forgetting. So many things must be going on.

I call my leader. She tells me to call seven times before giving up.

Seven times?

Is this real life? That sounds psychotic and aggressive.

But, she's the leader. So I do it. Seven times over the next three weeks.

I literally leave seven messages. Can you imagine? Just to be a fly on the wall at her house.

She's at her house saying, "Oh, that darn chick from the bank again … Will she ever quit?"

And I wait for a month. No callback. NOTHING. EVER.

Like, she NEVER EVER calls me back. Can you imagine this?

I'm deflated. And I can't tell my mom because she'll say, "I told you it's really hard, honey."

Besides, I don't want her to worry about me.

Either way, all that courage and energy I mustered up at the bank comes crashing down. I feel like I've been dumped by a dude. My heart hurts.

That night, I go and buy Ben & Jerry's™ ice cream. You know, the Chocolate Chip Cookie Dough. That stuff is legit.

I also pick up some chocolate syrup and whipped cream. I sit down on the couch that night with a spoon and a pint of ice cream. I spray the whipped cream on top and cover it in chocolate syrup while drowning in my sorrows.

I accidentally eat the whole pint.

I start rehearsing really bad thoughts in my head. *I can't possibly be good at this. Talking to people is super hard. I'm probably not meant for this because it feels uncomfortable. It's easier to just not do it and keep my stupid job.*

These thoughts destroy me.

But my mom always taught me during tough times to sleep on it, and it would be better in the morning.

Interestingly, the next day, I am hopeful again.

I hop on the company website and try to find my way into top leaders' private websites to learn as much as I can. I study and learn, but realize everyone has a different way of doing it.

I end up getting confused. And a confused mind does … nothing.

I call my recruiter and ask if she can help. She says that she knows we can do a scavenger hunt in the mall and meet new women.

We will take a clipboard, and if we find a woman with blonde hair, we will go up to her and tell her she's on my scavenger hunt checklist. And then, we will get her to book an appointment with us.

Sounds easy enough.

We head to the mall. My hands start sweating.

My mind is racing. *I can't do this. I can't do this.*

But I see my recruiter doing it and she's starting to WIN and get more points than me.

I don't like losing, so I finally approach someone.

And, like a gift from God, this lady says to me, "I would love to have you come to my house and host a party, and I'll invite all my friends! I would love that! Let's pick a date."

That NEVER happens. But it happened to me.

I'm so excited. We set a date. She is SO HAPPY. I am SO HAPPY. We even HUG.

But, I get home, and like a lunatic, for some reason, I get so nervous about this upcoming party.

I put off calling her for 10 days. And then, I put it off for 20 days, and then the day before the party, I decide to call her.

She's mad at me.

She never heard from me.

She never invited anyone.

She didn't think the party was happening.

And she hangs up on me.

I die. Dead.

And that's how I spend the first 365 days in my business. Loserville. But I'm still dreaming.

Year 2

I am still dreaming about this business every day while I work my day job. Dreaming big dreams.

I'm obsessing over the idea of success with this.

And now I have one-year-old $3,000 inventory on my shelf. I use $200 myself and give some to my roommate to use. The stuff is really good, like, I believe everyone should use this stuff, it's so good.

I call the company to figure out if this stuff has gone bad.

Good news. It has a three-year shelf life.

Good, I have two more years to figure this out.

It's a sunny Friday morning, and I'm having one of those larger than life, ultra-positive days.

I get into a really great conversation with the sweetest lady at a doctor's office. She's the receptionist.

She's so nice to me that I decide to ask her if she will host a party for my "new" business, and she actually agrees.

Then she actually holds it.

She invites two of her friends, and we all gather in her tiny kitchen around a small table.

I sell $197 and feel so proud of myself. That same lady even joins my team the next day.

I knew I could do it. I am on top of the world.

I invite her to the hotel event so she can get obsessed like I am.

It's magical. She has a great time.

We are new besties on a mission together.

And she never, ever, ever returns my calls ever again.

Ever.

I am deflated. What on earth.

And that's how year two goes. #WINNER

Year 3

It's fine. I call that girl 20 times and she never calls me back. Whatever. So weird. How could she not love this like I love it?

Wah.

I call my mom. She tells me in not so many words, "I told you so ..."

And I tell her I really believe in this, and I want to make this work.

Then, my mom agrees to host a party. A Pity Party, if you will.

Now, my mom isn't the type who typically has people over, so this is a BIG deal. She agrees to help me and invites five ladies she sort of knows from the office.

When they arrive, it's clear they only "sort of" know each other.

It's awkward. And I'm the leader in charge of making everyone become friends.

No pressure.

I am so nervous. I start my presentation with, "I'm so nervous. Sorry if I mess up." Then I continue the presentation with lots of umms, sorry's, and I don't know's.

My mom tells me later that I need to leave the sorry's out, and just roll with it. I was doing great other than that part.

Noted. Thanks, Mom.

I sell some, recruit no one.

And then, I'm back to square one. Uhhh ... now what.

A month later, I catch a break.

I am visiting my dentist for a checkup when I meet a nice lady named Sarah. She compliments my look and asks what products I am using. I tell her.

She tells me she lost her rep, wants to buy more products, and asks if I can help her.

Like, duh, of course I can. Rep of the year ... here I am. Someone get me a crown.

Naturally, I get her a catalog out of my car (an old catalog from two years ago) and hand it to her.

She orders $200 of product on the spot.

Sarah is a dream.

She is loyal.

She trusts my expert opinion.

She always wants the latest and greatest.

And Sarah single-handedly keeps my business afloat.

She orders from me even when I'm not "active," forcing me to get active and back into action.

She keeps ordering even when I don't believe this will ever get off the ground.

Every three months for the next 14 years, she orders from me.

Since I never want to disappoint my ONE client who thinks I'm the BEST rep of all time, I never give up.

And, gosh darnit, one day I *will* be the best rep of all time.

Everyone needs a Sarah.

If you haven't found her yet, find a Sarah. A Sarah will keep your business alive. More importantly, a Sarah will keep your hope alive.

Without Sarah, I'm not sure what my life would look like today.

Year 4

Sarah keeps my business afloat.

And I believe God placed her in my life so I wouldn't quit because he has a bigger plan for my life. He wants this to work for me.

Reaching the breaking point of utter boredom in my life and my sadness over my unfulfilled dream with $2,500 of unsold and expired inventory, I decide to switch things up.

One evening in my cold, Massachusetts apartment, I hop on a roommate website, do a search in California, and randomly find an old friend from college looking for a roommate in Costa Mesa.

What are the chances?

We connect. I take this as a sign that I need to move.

Almost immediately, I up and quit my job, land a new job as a uniform sales rep for high-end hotels, and move to California alone, as a 26-year-old.

Nuts.

I bring along all my expired inventory and store it in a closet in my new apartment. Three other roommates and I all pack into an apartment together because the rent is really high. So I squish that inventory in the corner.

Once moved in, I start my day job which ends up being 80+ hours a week and super intense.

Then, I attend some local meetings for my network marketing company and meet one friend at the new consultant orient-ation they hold in town.

I am so excited. We can build this together.

But a few weeks later, she decides it's dorky and quits.

I quit that year with her, too. I mean ... *I'm not trying to be a dork.*

Except, I don't quit on Sarah. I am the best rep ever to Sarah.

Year 5

I call my leader and explain how this isn't working.

Oh, and yes, this is year five. Just to be clear. For five years this madness has gone on.

I really want to make it work, but I just don't want to walk up to strangers. I'm in a new town, and I don't know anyone.

She recommends I start chatting with people and building friendships.

Nice idea, yet I ignore her advice and do nothing.

Then, I ignore her calls for the rest of the year.

She's literally the nicest lady ever. I'm just crazy. Clearly.

I work 80 hours a week at my new job selling uniforms. I earn a six-figure income. I also get recognized as being a top uniform seller and earn an all-expense-paid trip to tropical Aruba. I bring my long-distance boyfriend who is in Ohio.

I end up marrying that boy later in the story.

I'm doing well at work but also killing myself to make it happen putting in 80-hour workweeks.

I throw myself so much into work, so I can ignore the dream I have in my heart.

I know I am made for more. I know I am called to greatness. But I just can't do it.

I just can't. What's wrong with me?

And then Sarah orders again. I never send Sarah expired items. I only order new stuff for her from the company. Because I am, after all, the rep of the year.

Year 6

I really, really want to make my network marketing business work. I really do. But this inventory is six years old. It's all expired.

I still use the expired items for me. They are useless otherwise.

After all, I did pay for this stuff. And, I find they are actually still effective.

Maybe they don't really expire.

A risk I'm willing to take. It is $3,000 after all.

Things get serious with my long-distance boyfriend of two years, so I move to Ohio to live with him.

And I drive from California to Ohio with my expired inventory in my trunk.

Someone cue the theme song, "Let It Go ... Let It Go ...."

Get a grip, Michelle. This stuff is expired.

But, I hold onto the dream.

I shovel my expired inventory into a small cabinet in the apartment in Cleveland, Ohio. And I dust it off a bit.

Then, I head to Walmart® to grab a laminator.

This is going to be my big year. The breakout year of my network marketing business.

To get ready, I decide to print every idea off Google for my business.

And I spend evenings laminating the ideas and three-hole-punching them and putting them into binders. I do this for two months straight.

And I show my binders to my boyfriend.

I want to show him how serious I am about this business.

I am going to make it big this year. I'm going to study, learn, practice, and do this.

And then, this happens …

My boyfriend Brian and I go on a little weekend vacation. On the airplane, I sit next to a top commercial real estate agent, and he tells me that he is killing it making tons of money in real estate and that I should sign up with his company.

I take this as a sign.

So I get off the plane and get my real estate license in Ohio and decide to start selling commercial real estate because I met a dude on a plane who said it was a good idea.

I close a few deals, make a few bucks, and then the market crashes. Real estate is now dead. I miss the bubble.

It's 2009.

I am 100% commission based. And, now I have no income at this stupid job.

Thanks, dude on the plane.

And now, I need to make money.

Chapter 3 | Key Lessons:

- **Never quit.** If you get that icky feeling in your stomach that says this doesn't feel right, ask yourself this: *Does it not feel right because you haven't learned how to succeed yet?* Challenge yourself to find some success before deciding it's not for you.

- **Get comfortable with being uncomfortable.** It might feel like this is the hardest thing you have ever done. Welcome to entrepreneurship. You need to experience that difficulty to experience growth.

- **Don't go it alone.** Entrepreneurship is a road less traveled, but it's not a road you ever need to travel alone. Thanks to social media, you can join groups of like-minded women who are on the same journey. I have an online community that will cheer you on, uplift you, and give you new, amazing, big-thinking friends. Join here:

  DoItAnywayGirl.com/Club

- **Not everyone starts confident.** If you aren't confident, great! That's how you start. Your confidence is built through action and repetition.

- **Slow starts are relatable.** If you've had a slow start, great! That will make for a great story one day that others can relate to. Don't be ashamed of your story, for one day, it will inspire others.

- **Find a Sarah.** Truly. Find someone who just loves your products and orders from you regularly enough that it just doesn't make sense to quit. It's very hard to quit when you have someone counting on you. And consider that person a sign that you are meant to do MORE with this.

- **Don't buy a laminator and laminate ideas.** I was a lunatic. Clearly. That was a bad idea. But gosh, it was fun. One could say I have a laminator addiction. Even today.

- **Don't listen to a dude on a plane.** That's all.

Chapter Four

How to Talk about Your Network Marketing Business with Other Humans without Feeling Like an Alien

y boyfriend and I move into a new house together.

At this point, I decide: No more taking advice from dudes on planes.

I'm 29.

And I have a bigger dream for my life than working for someone else.

But I am frozen in fear.

My friend Erika pops over to see the new house. As I'm showing her my office, she spots all my inventory in a pile. I am in the middle of organizing it in my new office.

She says, "You sell this stuff? I've always wanted to try it." I explain it's a bit expired, but I can order some new, and she can pop over and try it. She's excited. She's a makeup counter sales rep for Chanel®, so she knows what good products are.

The products arrive and we get together and she tries the stuff and instantly falls in love. She purchases $300 worth. I'm blown away.

But I'm more blown away when, after using the products for just one week, she claims it is "hands-down the best product" she has ever used and she has never looked better. It's even better than Chanel.

And then, she says this: "I think I want to sell this instead."

I die.

You want to JOIN my team?

She does.

She quits Chanel on the spot and joins my team.

Now I have an excited team member, and I am clueless, so I decide to look up the local reps online who work for my network marketing company.

I stumble upon a lady who is about 20 years older than I am, and she appears to be very successful.

Her name is Maggie.

In a moment of courage, I send her an email and ask if she has a local meeting I can attend because I have a new team member.

Maggie replies back that she does, and she would love to have me.

The meeting is Monday evening, and it's at her house at 6 p.m.

Monday arrives and I let my boyfriend know I am going to make this business work. I am going to a meeting. I go alone before bringing my new rep there because I want to scope it out first.

And these ladies are so welcoming, loving, kind, and caring. I love them. I feel instantly at home.

They tell me to come back to training next week because they will show me the ropes.

The next week rolls around, and I don't go.

Partially because I feel like a burden since I am not part of their team. They are just doing me a favor.

And partially because this business has caused me so much overthinking and pain, I just want it to go away.

Then, this one thing happens that changes the trajectory of my life forever.

My phone rings.

It's Maggie. The BIG leader lady.

She says, "We missed you last night. Not sure where you were, but we really were hoping you'd come back next week. Can you make it?"

First thought: *I can't believe you care that much.*

Second thought: *I love you.*

I show up the following week, and I bring Erika along.

Erika loves it like I love it. It's so refreshing. And she sticks with selling for almost a year before moving away and starting another venture. But we have tons of fun trying to figure this thing out together.

And what's interesting about Maggie is that she doesn't even make a penny in helping us. We are not on her team.

Essentially, she's a good human.

That evening, because I was a leader with a team member, Maggie puts me in charge of the guests. My job is to greet them, get them water, and get them set up for the event. She trusts me, which tickles me because she is such a big deal.

Now, I may know how to talk to humans, but I don't know how to talk to humans about my own business. Yet.

As I'm leaving that night, Maggie hands me the script for the party and says, "Learn this. You are in charge of the guests next week."

I can't believe it, but I'm not about to let her down.

I am ready for a change.

I am emotionally drained from my corporate job.

I am tired of the office drama and the politics.

I'm not making money in this dead real estate market.

I am exhausted from all my overthinking for six years.

And I need a change.

Essentially, I am FED UP ENOUGH.

I just need one little nudge to get me going.

And Maggie gives me just that.

I tell her about how I have been stuck for six years, but I genuinely believe I can succeed at this.

She says one thing that night that sticks with me forever: "You know what Michelle? Successful women feel the fear and do it anyway."

Hmm ... I never thought of it that way.

But she isn't wrong.

No matter what, they still do it anyway. Hmm ... Maybe I should try that.

I leave that night with a new thought.

And a feeling in my heart that this woman is going to change my life forever.

The Fire That Changes Everything

After that meeting, I boldly announce to my boyfriend that I am going to quit my commercial real estate job officially.

It's not making me any money.

Literally, I am making zero dollars.

Plus, driving to a building 30 minutes away every day is costing me more in gas, so it is technically a negative business venture.

I am making negative $25 per week. That's even worse than zero dollars.

Either way, he looks worried.

First, I had told him I was going to make it BIG with the real estate thing. That didn't happen.

Then I told him I was going to make it BIG with this network marketing thing that I have failed at for six years. And that clearly wasn't happening.

Okay, so his hesitation is warranted.

He recommends I get a real job.

And I recommend he give me six months to prove myself. If it doesn't work out, I'll go back to the grind.

He agrees.

Oh, SHOOT. Did he just agree?

Ahh.

I have six months to hit a goal.

I have six months to make it work.

I have six months before I have to go back to 9-to-5 jail.

I have six months to PROVE MYSELF.

The FIRE under my BUTT was LIT.

But I can tell he doesn't believe I can do it.

My mom is also concerned about me.

My friends stop asking about what I've been up to because they just assume I am nuts at this point. I'm a jobless weirdo with a college degree.

I basically have no cheering squad.

But for some reason, that FIRES ME UP.

The second that someone else thinks I can't do something, I DO IT.

The next week, Maggie has another meeting, and that night, I have to present to all the guests. The good news is that it forces me to learn that presentation really quickly.

I remember thinking, *Lady, I have no clue what I'm doing. I'm a six-year failure with expired inventory. Dusty, expired inventory.*

I spend the entire week practicing on my boyfriend and talking out loud in the car. I speak that presentation over and over from the sheets she gave me.

I become obsessed with learning and perfecting it. And, of course, I nail it. Which earns me a weekly spot in helping at all her events. Which catapults my self-esteem.

Maybe I can do this.

A good lesson in Leadership 101: When you do for others what they can do for themselves, you take away their self-esteem. Maggie was a self-esteem creator.

[NOTE: If you are wishing you could have a Maggie in your life, I've got something for you! My passion is to give you a supportive and loving community with lots of cheerleaders (including me) that's totally free. You don't need my Maggie to be successful, you just need a supportive, loving community that cheers you on to achieve greatness. Join our club here: DoItAnywayGirl.com/Club.]

As I am leaving her house, in a quick two-minute conversation, she recommends I get rid of the dusty inventory and start over. Buy new inventory and treat it like a real business this time.

Hmm ...

So that night, I take my credit card and invest another $3,600. This time, I'm ALL IN. I don't tell anyone about my investment because, at this point, they already think I'm crazy.

But now, I am FULLY COMMITTED.

There is NO WAY, NO HOW that I won't make this work.

This is my full-time job. This is my commitment.

Remember, I'm new to town. I don't know anyone here. If I want to invite 20 people, I have to go meet them in the world.

Now that this is my full-time commitment, I start to treat it like a real job. I start thinking that if I take the 80 hours a week I was killing myself for someone else's company, why can't I do that for my own company?

The year is 2009.

The next day, I wake up, crush a hard workout, and then head to a networking event I find on Meetup.com.

It's at the Holiday Inn. And there will be over 100 people there.

I am scared. Very scared. But I have six months to prove I'm unafraid and actually awesome.

I remind myself the entire morning that successful women feel the fear and do it anyway.

Do it anyway, girl, I keep chanting inside my head.

I say it over and over. And I remind myself, my only job today is to go out and meet friends.

The introvert in me doesn't like going to find new friends because what if they don't like me, but the businesswoman in me decides to be assertive.

I have a point to prove.

WATCH ME.

At the event, I meet tons of friendly people.

Here's the truth about networking events. They are a dream come true for introverts because all the people who go to those things are extroverts and they all want to be your friend.

I make new friends, and I barely mention my network marketing business because again, that's not my style.

But, at the event, I follow the rules outlined in the book *How to Win Friends and Influence People*, which states that people just really like to talk about themselves, so when you get them talking, they will like YOU more.

Simple enough for me as an introvert. Make you talk more so I can talk less and you will like me more. Wow. Love it. Just my style.

Before leaving each conversation, I ask each new friend for their business card so they can keep me posted on other networking events. After all, I am new to the area and looking to meet more friends.

Then, I hop in my car. I take all these business cards back to my house.

A big pile of 30 cards.

And now, I am going to be SMART and ASSERTIVE.

One by one, I shoot them a quick personalized email saying something like this:

> *Hey Sally,*
>
> *It was super great to connect with you at the Holiday Inn networking event today. Loved learning about your insurance business and I will definitely refer you to people I meet along the way. I just loved your story about your dog, Jeffrey. Just so adorable!*
>
> *Keep me in your thoughts if you hear of new networking events coming up, as I'd love to join you and meet more people. This whole networking thing is new to me. I was actually nervous to attend, but you made me feel at home. So thanks for that.*
>
> *Also, not sure if you'd be interested, but I am putting together a networking portfolio of entrepreneurs at the top*

of their game in the area. And I'd love to feature you. Basically, we get together for an hour, you get to use some products from [Company Name] and we do before and after photos. Let me know if you'd like more details.

Again, super great to be connected. Hope to see you at another event soon!

Michelle

Guess what? Some people reply to me! Yes, real LIVE people respond to me asking for more information. Out of the 30, five message me back.

I die with excitement. I am a total rockstar.

I reply with this:

So great! Let's do this.

Okay, so how this works is we will get together at your place or mine and I'll customize the perfect products for you and we will recreate your look.

Then we will do some fun headshots with our phones. I'll send you those images after. It's all for free. And I'll put them in a book for all entrepreneurs to see who participate.

I hold these on Tuesdays and Thursdays at noon or 2 p.m. Which works best for you?"

Strategic. I give her two options ONLY. That's what Maggie recommends.

And she replies.

So I confirm her appointment with something like this:

Okay, fabulous.

You are all set for Tuesday, November 10th, from 2 p.m. to 3 p.m. at my home studio located at 11 Main Street in Anyville.

And, I actually just checked my datebook and I still have three openings during that time slot, so if you know any other businesswomen who might like a new headshot and to try some new products, let me know ASAP and I'll save those spots for them.

And, this is totally free of charge.

Also, if you do fall in love with something, I will have products available for sale but of course, there is no obligation.

Thanks so much for helping me put together my portfolio. You are such a blessing.

Michelle

That is how I book my first appointment.

By email.

Because I cannot talk to people about my business.

And I cannot call people.

Because I am, at this point, still a self-proclaimed introvert.

For the men I meet at the events, I just change the first script to this:

> *Hi Brad,*
>
> *It was super great to connect with you at the Holiday Inn networking event today. Loved learning about your insurance business and I will definitely refer you to people I meet along the way. I just loved seeing the photos of your kids. They are precious!*
>
> *Keep me in your thoughts if you hear of new networking events coming up, as I'd love to attend and meet more people. This whole networking thing is new to me.*
>
> *Also, not sure if you know any ladies who might be interested, but I am putting together a networking portfolio of female entrepreneurs at the top of their game in the area.*
>
> *Basically, we get together for an hour, they get to use some products from [Company Name] and we do before and after photos. Let me know if you know anyone that might benefit.*
>
> *Again, super great to be connected. Hope to see you at another event soon!*
>
> *Michelle*

And, it works on the men, too.

It's working!

In all honesty, I'm so excited, yet super surprised any of this is actually working. They're literally the littlest wins, but these wins are making me feel like the most powerful human ever.

I can go to a networking event.

I can talk to other humans at the event.

I can get their business cards.

I can email them.

And I can get responses.

I'm actually amazing. Maybe I can do this.

Chapter 4 | Key Lessons

- **If it's not working for you, try something different.** If you can't approach people, think about how you can email, text them, or use social media. I'll share some epic emails, texts, and social media strategies in upcoming chapters.

- **There is more than one way to make this industry work.** Don't believe that you have to do it just one way. Do it your way. Figure out what works for you.

- **If you are stuck, find a way to make it work for you at your current confidence level.** Sometimes, other network marketers with tons of confidence will convince you to do it their way. But if that shuts you down and you won't take action, find a more passive approach until you can do it at their level.

- **Small actions and wins will start to slowly build your confidence, so take the first step.** Take one little action each day to connect with a potential client or potential recruit, even if that scares you a little bit. But if you are stuck, and you don't know what to say, and you wish someone would just give you some simple, printable scripts that you could use immediately, let me just grant that wish right here: DoItAnywayGirl.com/Scripts.

- **Meeting humans isn't actually all that scary.** If you are conjuring up these crazy ideas that humans you will meet will bite your head off or be mean to you, it's actually very rare that will happen in person. So, just get out there and meet humans. They won't bite. Promise.

Chapter Five

Win the Ignore Game
with This Simple Strategy

I've got week one under my belt.

After my first networking event, I end up booking five people for appointments.

And that doesn't mean I send just one message and they book.

It takes much more than that. It's called persistence.

I have a strategy to make this happen which I'll share now.

Because I am on SUCH a mission, the ones who tell me they are interested go directly onto my "I'm Interested" list.

I keep it VERY organized in the notes section of my phone. I let no one fall through the cracks.

I only have six months. I have to be impeccable with every piece of this. This is my job for the next six months.

If you tell me you are INTERESTED, you better believe I will treat this as the opportunity of a lifetime that you absolutely have to experience.

Because I truly believe it is. And because I know each person I meet is like a little seed that I need to love so it can bloom.

Seeds need to be planted in soil, watered, and cared for to survive. *That's my job.* To treat each person like a little seed that needs love.

If I am sloppy with my leads (or seeds), and I let them drop on the ground and get stepped on and crushed, they will never bloom into what they were meant to bloom into. I take this job very seriously, protecting each seed that comes my way.

I offer women a chance to take a break from their mad lives and just relax for a moment and focus on themselves.

My service is something everyone must have.

I become obsessed with this idea from this point forward.

(I urge you to become obsessed with your mission and your calling to serve others.)

My mindset becomes this: *Okay, you are interested, then I will make sure I follow up and follow up again and get you booked. You deserve this. I know how busy you are. I will make sure we get you on our datebook. You need this service. You deserve this.*

I pretend I work for a hair salon or a spa, and I am the front desk receptionist.

So, when someone says, "Oh yes, that sounds amazing. I am totally interested. Let me get back to you ..."

I assertively say, as any good front desk receptionist would, "Okay! Sounds great. I'll check back in tomorrow. As of right now, I have openings next Tuesday at 2 p.m. or Thursday at 6 p.m. Let me know if either works, and I can secure those for you."

Always give two options. It's professional and helps people make an easy choice.

As promised, I follow up the next day—even though she hasn't replied back to me.

I mean, after all, she said she was interested. She was telling me there was a chance.

Until she tells me otherwise, I will follow up. That's called being ASSERTIVE.

There is a huge difference between being assertive and being pushy. And here's the difference:

Assertive is following up with someone who says they are interested but they aren't replying. They are simply busy. So follow up until they become a yes or a no.

Pushy is following up with someone who has said, "No, I am not interested." And then you continue trying to convince them to book an appointment with you.

No means no. "Let It Go ... Let It Go." Cue the song again.

Your ultimate goal with each and every client is to take them from an IGNORE to a YES or a NO. That's it.

As long as you are being IGNORED, you can follow up until you get that YES or NO. Because IGNORE is not a yes. And IGNORE is not a no.

IGNORE is just a sign that someone is busy.

Let's say you have someone who has expressed an interest in getting together or attending your event online.

It's totally fine to send a series of text messages or emails that look like this:

HER: YES, I'D LOVE THAT.

> *Day 1: Okay, sounds perfect. We can get you scheduled. Looks like I have Tuesday or Thursday open at 6 p.m. Would either of those work for you?*

HER: IGNORE.

> *Day 2: Hi Sarah, just wanted to check back in. Just finalizing my calendar for next week. Does next week work for you? I could do Tuesday or Thursday at 6 p.m. Would either of those work for you?*

HER: IGNORE.

> *Day 4: Hi there! I know you wanted to get together for the [whatever thing] I am putting together so I have you on my list. I just wanted to check back. I have an opening left for Thursday at 6 p.m. and also Saturday at noon. And if now isn't a good time, I'll check back in a few days. Does either work for you?*

HER: IGNORE.

> *Day 7: Hey, girlfriend. I know you were interested, but I don't want to bug you. Is now not a good time?*

HER: IGNORE.

> *Day 10: I haven't heard back, so I will check back in a few weeks. I still have you on my list for the [whatever thing], and if you're not interested, just let me know. Sound good?*

NOTE:

- Every single statement ends with a question. Why? Because in a text, people reply to questions. It tells them the next logical step to take.

- Every single statement is short and to the point. Why? Because people text too much. Keep it simple and easy to read and reply to. Less is always more.

- Always give TWO options when getting someone scheduled. It clears the clutter in their brain, lets them easily check two dates in their calendar, and get back to you. One of the worst things you can say is, "I'm totally open. What works for you?" Imagine if your doctor said he was "totally open and you could come in anytime." Horrifying. Worst doctor EVER. Don't be the worst *rep* ever.

With this as my strategy, that first week I book five of them and sell to four of them.

I have all brand new inventory, so I am super motivated to sell it.

I also feel super professional.

And they are impressed. One lady tells me how nice it is to be able to take everything home that she wants right away. She loves it. She recommends me to her friend who books an appointment the following week.

Dude, I'm like rep of the year officially now.

Glad I got rid of the dusty expired inventory. Gosh, did that weigh me down. I had a weird addiction to taking it everywhere with me.

Now, I'm feeling more confident because:

- I've met strangers.

- I've booked strangers.

- I've become friends with strangers.

- I've sold to strangers.

Wow, I can do this again next week.

That's the biggest lesson from this chapter.

Get yourself that SMALL win.

Because if you can meet a stranger, book a stranger, become friends with a stranger, and sell to the stranger, you can do it over and over and over.

You can do it in person. You can do it online. *You can do it.*

Get that first win.

It's the hardest, but the most important.

Because it can get you unstuck.

Because you can always find another stranger.

Once you have that, you know you can do this.

Chapter 5 | Key Lessons

- **Keep all your potential clients organized.** The key to success is never letting any lead fall through the cracks. Protect them like they are a little seed that needs to be planted, watered, and nurtured.

- **Be obsessed with the idea you offer a service the world needs.** You are not selling a product. You are here to change the world and impact lives for the better. So, go out with a loving heart and serve.

- **Follow-up is the name of the game.** Your job is to be a professional reminder. Yes, that's your new title: Professional Reminder.

- **There is a difference between being assertive and being annoying.** Don't be annoying.

- **End all text messages with a question if you warrant a reply.** People are busy. They don't have time to think. Get to the point and end it with a question they can quickly reply to.

- **Get a small win by selling to a stranger.** Because once you do it once, you will now have the confidence and ability to do it again.

Chapter Six

How to Find Leads FAST with the Fabulous Referral Game

*N*ow, I must find more strangers.

I continue with my strategy of attending networking events, meeting people, and emailing them.

I do this for a solid month. Day in and day out.

Because I know it works.

Why would I change it?

I keep doing it.

But, there is a part of me that keeps thinking, *Now, how can I make this better? More powerful? More productive? More successful?*

So, one night while listening to a call being hosted by a top seller in the company, I have an epiphany.

This sweet little lady with a southern accent explains her strategy for getting referrals at her in-person appointments.

She says, "Well, you see y'all, what I've been doing at all my appointments is I ask them to give me referrals. I ask for them to flip over their customer sheet and write the names of 20 friends that would like to have an appointment like this. And I make it a contest, and I give a prize away to the person who gives me the most names."

I hear that idea and get excited.

I can't believe that actually works because I would never give out my friends' names, but I'm going to do this.

And that night while in bed, I can't sleep.

So I get up and head to my computer, and I think that it would be really smart to have an actual sheet I have people fill out.

I type at the top of my sheet:

The Fabulous Referral Game

I think, *Good title. I mean, who wouldn't want to play a fabulous game. Perfect.*

Now, I'll add 20 lines for names and cell phone numbers. Throw a pink border on it plus a few pink crowns.

Then, I add this:

> *When you list the names and phone numbers of your friends or family members, they will receive a fabulous free [whatever session].*
>
> *CONTEST: Be the FIRST to fill in all lines and win a fabulous gift!*

And at the bottom I write:

Please be assured that I treat each friend or family member with the utmost care and respect! Thank you for supporting my small business!

I leave a field for their full name and the date.

And I look at it and think, *Good enough. Let's try this out tomorrow.*

I print 20 copies. And head back to bed. This is the actual flyer I created that night:

63

The next day, my guests arrive at my door.

At this point, I'm about 30 days in and I start to realize, if I have people come to me instead of me going to meet them, I can see more people in a day. It is more productive. So I stop offering to come to them and just offer my place.

NOTE: Obviously, you know your situation best, so if you can only travel, only offer that.

For this appointment, I decide to play my new, freshly-printed referral game.

I play it toward the end of the appointment when they like me.

They first have to figure out if they like me. They never like me when they first sit down. But once they do like me, they are open to playing this game.

So, I play after they have experienced the products and feel happy, but before I offer to sell them anything. It's the perfect stopping point in the party.

Then, I say this:

> *I have to do 100 appointments this month to help me earn my [insert your tangible goal like a car or vacation], and if you know anyone that would enjoy a free session just like what you are getting today, then put their name and number on this Fabulous Sheet.*
>
> *If I should text them, circle "text" or if I should call them, circle "call."*
>
> *And it's a race, so whoever finishes first with the most points wins a prize out of my prize basket.*

Oh! And you get triple points for people over age 25. So just put a star next to those people.

Ready to play? Using your cell phone isn't cheating. Ready, set ... go!

Then, my job is to be SILENT.

IMPORTANT TIP #1: Seriously, do not talk to or even disturb someone giving you referrals. EVER. *They will stop writing.* I've tested it. They put down their pen to talk to you. And then you cry inwardly because you can think of no good way to get them to pick up their pen again and start writing.

IMPORTANT TIP #2: I included the over age 25 bonus because sometimes you get a younger crowd, who refers you to a younger crowd, who refers you to a younger crowd. So, that will get you back to adults. You can also set a requirement that they need to be over the age of 18.

What is the prize they get for being the winner?

I give away a beautifully-wrapped, 50¢ hand cream. They don't know it's 50¢. It looks like it's $5.

Make a big deal of whatever you give and they will absolutely go bonkers for it!

It's more about celebrating the win and making them feel special versus the price you paid for the gift.

You are running a business. Be smart about your expenses.

Poor people get poor by living like they are rich. Rich people get rich by living like they are poor. Less is more.

Back to the story. I play the game. And the five women I see that day give me 75 names total—75 names! I am dying with excitement.

I start to think that if I just did this at each appointment, gone would be the days of going to networking events. I realize how HUGE this is.

Now I have to prove I can get them to book an appointment with me.

But, I wouldn't dare pick up the phone.

Hmm … Let me put on my introverted unicorn hat. Let me come up with a plan for my introverted self.

TEXT!

Oh, yes, I can text them.

I'm a wizard at texting. So that's what I do.

That same night, before 8:30 p.m., I text the referral this:

> *Sarah,*
>
> *Jessica Smith recommended to text you. I need to do 100 free [insert special service] for a [Company Name] contest. Any interest in a free [insert special service]?*
>
> *Michelle*

Then, the next reply was always this:

Yes! When?!

or

Okay, tell me more.

or

No thanks.

Then, my second text is:

We can pick a one-hour window that works best for you. And you get a fabulous _____ treatment, a [name another treatment], plus [awesome other treatment]. I have Mondays & Saturdays open. What's best for you?

Then, the third text that I send is:

Okay, would Monday, May 5th at 11 a.m. or 3 p.m. work better for you?

Then, we may have several more texts, but the final text that seals everything is ...

Can I get your email so I can send you a confirmation? Or I can text you a confirmation with the details. What's best?

The last text I send is:

Oh, and can you give me a 48-hour notice if you need to reschedule?

I'm in a contest, and I have to have these [name of

treatment] done, so I'm saving the spot just for you. Oh, and it looks like I still have openings for 3 more during that time slot.

Let me know ASAP if anyone else would like to come with you and I'll save those seats for you.

The confirmation email I send is:

Hi Amber! You are confirmed for Friday, May 19th, from 7 to 9 p.m. This time is reserved for you plus up to three friends for a [whatever session]. Please let me know 48 hours in advance if you need to cancel.

During your appointment, you can expect: A fabulous _____ treatment, a [name another treatment], plus [awesome other treatment].

My Address: 123 Main Street, Anytown, MA—See you on the 19th!

Michelle

Company Name

Cell Phone

Email

I test this puppy out on that first group.

The results are astounding. I send out 75 messages and I book 7 people.

STOP IT. I am so excited.

I call Maggie and announce the news about the Fabulous Game. We schedule calls with our teams and share it with everyone who asks about it.

It goes viral to tons of other teams.

Over the years, my cheesy Fabulous sheet has been upgraded and adapted into much cuter versions all over the web.

Either way, it WORKS. And that's what matters!

Now I realize if I get at least 50 names a day, I can average 5 new appointments booked, so I can always see 100 new clients per month.

Here's how the numbers shake out:

- Out of every 10 referrals I am given, two say yes.

- Of the two, one books and shows up.

- One says a firm no.

- And 7 ignore me. They disappear into lost unicorn land. Not sure where they go.

But I don't even need to worry about the lost unicorns because guess what? I am so busy with all the new unicorns who are showing up. Essentially, out of every 10 names I get, I will meet one new person.

At this point in the story, I now know how to meet strangers and multiply the strangers into more and more without leaving my home.

If I ever run out of referrals, I know how to meet a new stranger at a networking event. I am starting to feel super confident about this whole thing.

Baby steps. I am growing. I am getting there.

I am feeling proud of myself. I'm making money. I'm paying off my inventory.

But, I have five months left.

I gotta kick it up a notch and build another income stream.

I need to learn how to recruit.

Chapter 6 | Key Lessons

- **Never stop learning.** I learned about the Fabulous Game because I attended a phone call training one evening. That game skyrocketed my business. I'm glad I attended that training.

- **The right script matters.** With the right script, I was able to quickly, assertively, and easily book new strangers. Want to print my scripts so you can easily refer to them later? Here you go!

DoItAnywayGirl.com/Scripts

- **Warm leads are always easier than cold leads.** Referrals are warm leads. They will book with you much easier when their friend has referred them. There is safety in your friend referring you to something she enjoyed.

- **Always be prepared with lots of Fabulous sheets printed.** Never run out of the game sheet when you are with people. I would personally print 500 at a time on light pink paper with black ink. That was the cheap way to do it. White paper with black ink is the cheapest.

Chapter Seven

The Magical Team-Building Formula

I am making pretty good money just selling the products in my first month. I make a 50% commission, so I use some to pay down my inventory and the rest to live on. It's working.

But, I know that this opportunity can help other people change their situation, so I want to share it with them.

I also know that by sharing it with them, I will earn a commission check for their success.

To me, it just seems like a win/win. Help others make more. Personally make more money.

But, I'm not sure how to recruit people.

I do some digging online and learn that if someone LOVES the products, then that person is a great candidate to invite to join the company.

Got it. Get clients. Have them fall in love with the products. Invite them to hear more.

I've got 100 new clients I've met. Some bought, some didn't. I'll test it out on them.

My script:

> *Hi Sarah!*
>
> *So fun getting together yesterday.*
>
> *Wondered if you'd be interested in meeting for coffee to hear a little bit more about making extra money with [Company Name]?*
>
> *I think you have an amazing energy that people are drawn to and would love to give you the details.*
>
> *And even if it's not for you, I'll treat you to a fun coffee drink ... You can even get a good one with whipped cream. Whatcha think?*

I send it to everyone I've met so far that I'd like to have on my team. (Honestly, not EVERYONE.) I pick the ones I would feel safe to spend the night in a hotel room with at company events and people I would be proud to introduce to my mentor Maggie.

I also start to send it to everyone I meet within 24 hours of meeting me.

This is the only way I know how to recruit at this point in my journey.

And, guess what? 15 people of the 100 agree to meet with me.

My plan for each woman is this:

Before meeting with her and treating her to coffee, I ALWAYS have her watch a video on YouTube about the company opportunity. I find a ton of different and amazing leaders from the company on YouTube, choose the most inspiring story, and share that story with her.

I know that it will add another layer of proof that this is a great way to make money. Because when you *do* work it, you *do* make money. *I am making money.* After paying off all my expenses for my first month and paying down some of my inventory, I've already profited $1,000 in my first month.

Now, that's a far cry from the six-figure income I was making, but I am willing to take a pay cut just to have my freedom back and to build my own business that can grow exponentially higher.

Either way, I let that video do all the work for me.

I say:

> *Great, that day/time sounds good. I'll see you then. Oh, and let me send you a video you can watch before we meet … it's about 15 minutes long so you can see a little more about [Company Name] too. :)*

Will they watch it? Some will. Some won't. The ones who do are the ones who come charged with excitement about the possibilities they're beginning to see for themselves. I'm about to show them what's possible—even if they're introverted like me.

Chapter 7 | Key Lessons

- **Ask them.** It's just that simple. Ask people to hear more about your opportunity. It will surprise you how many people will be open to hearing a new way to make extra money.

- **Keep it cool.** Sometimes we think we have to be all salesy and weird. Just be you and invite people to meet you for coffee. Some will meet you just out of curiosity.

- **Send them some information to watch before you meet.** Why? Because otherwise, they will go Googling to find their information and that can be a dangerous road for them to go down. Every company has someone who had a bad experience and took that ugly message of failure to the internet.

- **Build a team and build residual income.** There is power that exists in helping others to make a better living for their family. You can be a life-changer. Don't keep this a secret from others. It's your duty.

Chapter Eight

Meet for Coffee, Follow the Script, and Recruit (Sometimes)

*N*ow, I am at coffee.

I remember this vividly ... I'm meeting Sam. Starbucks. Table by the window. I buy her drink, which is a mochaccino with whipped cream on top.

I'm nervous.

But, I follow what I've found online.

I'm super casual in my conversation. We chit chat for five minutes about the day.

Then I say, "Okay, so here's my little guide that I'm supposed to follow along. Is that cool?"

Then I read from the guide.

I say, "First, I'm going to ask you a bit about you, so I get to know your story. Then, I can tell you a bit about my journey if I haven't already. Then, I'll answer any questions you have and give you more details. And then, I'll ask if this is something you want to do."

1. *What do you like the best about your job or situation right now?*

2. *Tell me about you, your family life, education, favorite things to do.*

3. *What would you change if you could change anything right now?*

4. *Based on your current goals and dreams, where do you see yourself five years from now?*

5. *If you could dream up the perfect career for you, what three things would be most important?*

6. *At this point in your life, what do you feel you need the most?*

 IMPORTANT TIP: God gave us two ears and one mouth for a reason. So I listen, write and listen, and write and listen.

I write all her answers down while she is talking. It makes her feel important and makes me look smarter when I reference it later in the conversation.

Now, I take what she has said for answers and include those in points in my story.

EXAMPLE:

If she says, "My perfect career would allow me to work from home, have time freedom, and get a company car," then you would touch on how you:

1. *Love working from home because of this career and don't have to feel stressed and rushed each morning.*

2. *Get to design your own life because you own your own business, so it feels free and happy each day.*

3. *Can earn a company car through the company car program, which is such an amazing perk. (And share a little flyer that shows the car options—if your company offers a car program.)*

Then, I say, "So, did I share my story with you already, or if you'd like, I can just tell you my quick, three-minute journey?"

Now, at this point in the game, I'm in month one of actually making money. I don't have much to share except this:

For me, I joined this company six years ago, and for six years, it was my backup plan. My Plan B.

At the time, I was selling pharmaceuticals and had a cushy job with a company car.

And I signed up at that time because I love the products, so I'd get a discount on everything, but more importantly, so I would have a backup plan in case my full-time job went south. I'm a single woman, and I believe every woman should have a backup plan—especially in today's tumultuous market.

And, that's what happened to me a month ago. I had switched careers a few times, was working as a commercial real estate agent, and just about a month ago, the real estate market crashed. I stopped making money. So, my Plan B quickly became my Plan A.

So, as the introvert I am, knowing no one in town, I learned how to meet people in town at networking events and became their friends. Then, I would email them, much like I did you, and let them try the products. And it worked. People started to buy from me and refer to friends. And I've already made an extra $1,000 in my first month.

So, while it wasn't what I was making before, I am so thankful I had a backup plan because it caught me when I needed it.

So, let me ask you this: If I only had five minutes to share some facts with you about our [Company Name Career], what would you be curious about?

Then I listen to her.

I'm nervous.

I try to answer her questions, but I'm nervous I'm saying things wrong. Yet, I calm myself down and remember that this is my first one and it is just practice.

Sam says outright, "I love your story. And this all sounds great, but I'm not interested in joining at all. But I am glad to at least have met you for coffee."

And there you have it.

"Wah!!!" I think in my head.

I ask her if she'd like to keep it in her back pocket as a Plan B?

Nope. No interest.

We part ways and I feel deflated, but then I change my thinking and do a little self-talk, *"Michelle, get over yourself. That was practice. Good practice. Get over it. Move on. You have 10 more to go."*

I'm actually glad I booked a handful on the same day. I know there is someone out there that needs this.

The next person I booked for two hours after Sam.

Her name is Rachel. I go through the same routine.

Then I say, "So, let me ask you this: If I only had five minutes to share some facts with you about our [Company Name Career], what would you be curious about?"

She asks me questions. This is a good sign.

I had stayed up late the night before and learned online that someone who is interested will always throw you an obstacle that you must overcome before she will join. So I practiced how to overcome them. (I've listed the typical objections and responses at the end of this chapter for you.)

Rachel throws me an objection and I overcome it. I nail it.

I answer her next question.

When there is silence for a second, I say this: "May I ask you a question? If you did this, what's the BEST thing that could happen to you?"

She answers. Then, she smiles. I can tell that she starts dreaming of a better life.

When there is more silence because I can tell she is on the fence about joining, I say this: "On a scale of 1 to 10, one being never in a million years and 10 being I want to sign up now, what is your interest level in joining this company?"

She says, "8."

I say, "What would bridge the gap to bring you from an 8 to a 10?"

And I overcome whatever obstacle she brings up.

Then I say, "Do you want me to show you what the sheet you sign up with looks like so you can see the details?"

She says, "Yes."

I show her the agreement to join.

I say, "This is the agreement. So basically, you'd fill this out and you can pick if you want [this product] or [that product] and the total comes to like $--- plus tax and shipping. So it's roughly $---. And if you didn't want to pay today, you can just pay whenever. You can put a card down, or write a check, and tell me to put it through on whatever day you want it to go through. In five days, your kit will arrive, and you'll have your own business from home."

I set a pen down in front of her on top of the agreement.

To my surprise, she grabs it and starts filling out the paper.

I die with excitement, but I play it cool.

I go silent.

I take a look at my datebook instead to distract myself.

She signs up. Day 30. I have my second team member that I recruited myself.

Okay, sweet. Now, I know how to recruit.

This same month, I continue the same process with everyone I've met thus far at my appointments, and by the end of my second month, I have built a team of 10 recruits.

SHUT UP.

I think I can do this.

I can meet strangers. I can sell to them. I can get referrals from them. I can recruit them.

Someone get me a crown or a unicorn to ride.

I am really feeling proud of myself.

What's next?!

At this point, you may be thinking, *Hey, Michelle, you promised you'd share those objections people have and how to overcome them.*

And you know what?

You'd be right!

As promised, here are the typical objections and how I learned to overcome them:

I don't have time.

Oh, I get it. I was the same way! If I could teach you how to earn an extra $100 to $200 per week working just three hours a week, could you find a few extra hours?

I don't have money.

That's why you need this! This can change everything. If I could show you how to earn your $100 back within two weeks, could you find someone to help you get started? If we could find you the $100, is this something you would like to try?

I'm not the sales type.

Ditto. I'm literally an introvert, so I know how you feel. What I found was that probably 90% of the women who start [Company Name] are not the sales type. If I could teach you how to show this product and let it sell itself—without being pushy—would you feel better about doing it?

Another angle for I'm not the sales type.

Can you describe a typical salesperson? (Let her answer. She will say things like loud, pushy, abrasive.) Did you think I was like that?

She will say, *"Of course not."*

You say, *"Cool. That's the kind of salesperson you can be."*

Mic Drop.

This essentially is where you take your microphone in the middle of the coffee shop and throw it on the ground while standing on the seat of your table. Just kidding. Don't do it, but pretend to do it in your mind.

I don't know anyone.

Ditto! I'm totally new to the area and started with no friends and no family, so I can show you how to build by meeting strangers you turn into friends. If I can teach you how to meet people, would you be game?

Or, you could also ask for that last objection, *"Do you want me to walk you through how I meet people locally as an introvert?"*

I need to talk it over with my family first.

What do you think they'll say?

Typically, she will respond with, *"Oh, they don't care what I do."*

I'm too shy.

Oh, I get it. I'm the same way. I'm an introvert. But, I knew I didn't want to be that way forever. For me, I was shy because I was insecure in myself. Would you be open to working with me, and I can show you how to overcome it? I see something special in you that reminds me of myself.

But I had a friend that did this and totally failed.

Oh, me too. It wasn't my friend's thing, either. I think there is probably someone in every single occupation on earth that hasn't done well while others did.

So, those are the most common objections you will hear. And if you make up some note cards and practice them for a few hours, you'll be in great shape to overcome any obstacles thrown your way. Seriously, if I can do this, you can too.

Chapter 8 | Key Lessons

- **Keep it cool at coffee.** Just be conversational and be a friend.

- **If you are nervous, bring a guide along.** Even as a top leader, I brought my guide along and wrote on it. Sometimes we have so much to remember ... So if that's one less thing to think about and you can use it as a reference while keeping it cool and conversational, do it!

- **Learn how to overcome objections.** I practiced them daily when I was getting ready in the morning. I'd say them out loud. It's amazing how you can build muscle memory in your brain just through repetition. Play every scenario out in your head and practice through it, so when it happens in real life, you are cool as a cat.

- **Some will, some won't, so what?** That was something my mentor always told me when I was sad someone didn't join my team. Not bad advice. If you work the numbers enough, it will all work out. More often than not, someone who isn't having success isn't asking enough people daily.

Chapter Nine

Exactly What to Say
and When to Say It

At this point in the game, the only things I really know how to do are:

1. Meet strangers

2. Book them for an appointment

3. Sell to them

4. Get referrals from them

5. Recruit them

And that's all you really need to know to be successful in this business.

Epiphany!

Honestly, that's it! I just need to stop overthinking it and do more of what I've been doing.

Maybe, just maybe, I can teach this to others. What I am doing is simple—even though I don't totally feel confident in my abilities.

I'm doing it afraid, but I'm doing it anyway.

And if my new recruits just do the same, they will get results.

So, I decide to teach them what I know.

I decide that every Tuesday and Thursday at 6 p.m., I'll host a live party at my home.

I'll call it "training," and my team can come and bring up to three guests for training.

That way, I can still get my appointments in for the week; while at the same time, I can train my new reps and they can learn the ropes. I always have my five personal guests at these events.

My new reps can invite a few extra friends, and we have a fun party together. I host these in my basement.

For my own business, I also personally hold a Super Saturday appointment at my home, which consists of three to five appointment time slots so I can see as many new personal clients as possible.

But I can't afford a new table at this point, so I just have guests sit around my pool table for the appointment.

I put a ping pong table cover over the pool table, and then cover it in a black, wrinkle-free stretch fabric. I throw some pink placemats on the table, some flowers, and a basket of wrapped gifts to make it look cute. I'm finding that only one rep out of my ten new reps is actually coming.

I share my concern and frustration with Maggie.

And she shares something that forever changes my thinking:

For every ten you recruit …

One will be your hotshot.

Three will be doing a little.

Three will be doing nothing.

And three will be quitting.

MIND BLOWN.

So not everyone will be a hotshot?

Ugh. Well, fine. That just means I need a team of 100 to find 10 hotshots.

Got it.

Keep working.

I just work with the ones who are showing up because I have five months to make this work.

Quite honestly, I don't have time to stop and wait for them to catch the vision.

For all I know, they are on "Michelle's Six-Year Sleeper Plan."

Since I know how NUTS that plan is, I'm not about to spend my time waking them up. I check in once a week and invite them to stuff. They ignore me.

I keep going. I focus on what I can control.

I remind myself that one person will not dictate my success.

Meet more strangers. Book strangers. Get referrals from strangers. Sell to them. Recruit them. Wash, Rinse, Repeat.

I am on a crazy mission, and I won't stop because my team isn't following along. I will show them the way. If it's to be, it's up to me.

For my one rep who is actually showing up, I teach her how to host a party.

This is what I teach her in real time:

It's 6 p.m. The doorbell rings. There is our first guest. I swing open the door. I greet her with a huge smile. I'm wearing a crisp, white dress with my company lab coat. My makeup is fresh and on point.

> *"Hi! What's your name? Sarah! Welcome, welcome! Come in! It's so great to have you. We are going to be downstairs, so we will get you all set up. Follow me!"*

I pick a seat for Sarah and ask her if she'd like some coffee, tea, or water, and I bring it to her. Then I hand her a customer information sheet to fill out and give her a pen.

> *"Just go ahead and fill this out while we wait for our other guests. And once you are done, just set your pen down and we will get you started with your [insert special name] treatment."*

NOTE: We always offer a little company pampering treatment when they first arrive, so if you have something simple that makes them feel great, offer that while you wait for other guests.

Other guests arrive and we go through the same motions while my new rep follows along. After the third guest, I have my new rep take over the door duty and take over the conversations.

I make sure all my products and documents are ready to go, and while doing so, I am never forgetting that the most important part of my job is to make everyone feel important.

I keep reminding myself, *This is not about me. This is about them. Women don't care how much you know until they know how much you care.*

Because I'm an introvert and small talk isn't always my gift, I basically rotate questions to get to know guests as they are arriving.

Sometimes the guests come with friends. Sometimes they are all strangers to one another.

I keep a little cheat sheet tucked next to my products that I can reference to make small talk easier:

- Are you guys from the area?

- How do you all know each other?

- What do you do for work?

- Do you have kids?

- Any fun weekend plans?

- Been on any fun vacations lately?

Then, once everyone has a drink, has filled out their customer sheet, and has had their treatment, I make sure they all have their products to use in front of them. Then, I begin my presentation.

PRESENTATION

Step One: Introductions

It's so great to have you all here! Let's go around and do introductions so we aren't a bunch of strangers staring at each other in a room together.

- *Tell me your name!*

- *What do you do for work?*

- *Something you're excited about in your life!*

Step Two: A Little About Me

Awesome to get to know you all! And real quick, I'll share my story so you know my background.

- *I have been building my business for this long …*

- *Before I started my business, this is my story …*

- *I never saw myself doing this because …*

- *I was attracted to this though because …*

- *The best part of it so far is …*

- *My current goal is …*

At this point in the game, my story is the same one I am telling at coffee appointments:

> *For me, I joined this company six years ago, and for six years, it was my backup plan. My Plan B.*
>
> *At the time, I was selling pharmaceuticals and had a cushy job with a company car.*
>
> *I signed up at that time to get a discount on everything because I love the products, but more importantly, so I would have a backup plan in case my full-time job went south.*
>
> *I'm a single woman, so I believe a man is not a backup plan and that every woman should have a Plan B— especially in today's tumultuous market.*
>
> *And, I'll be honest. That's exactly what happened to me a month ago. The real estate market crashed, and I stopped making money. My Plan B quickly became my Plan A.*
>
> *So, being the introvert I am, knowing no one in town, I learned how to meet people locally. And I've already made an extra $1,000 in my first month. Although it isn't what I was making before, I am so thankful I had a backup plan because it caught me when I needed it.*
>
> *Now, I am on a mission to earn a company car in the next four months so I don't have to go back to corporate America. I need to meet 100 new clients every single month to make that happen. So THANK YOU for being here and helping me on my mission!*

And I'd also like to introduce you to the amazing Lynn! She is NEW to the company and excited to build her business, so I'll have her share her story with you now.

(Prior to this, I explained to her how to share a short two-minute story.)

Step Three: Audience Interaction

- *Okay, let's jump in! Raise your hand if it's your first time using our products!*

- *If you have used our products, raise your hand if it's been more than three years since you've tried our NEW products! Okay, WOW. You are all in for a treat!*

Step Four: Our Company Is the BOMB

Now, before we jump in with the audience participation portion, I am going to share the top six reasons our company and products are absolutely the best for you.

- **Reason 1: Speak to Your Audience | Why Your Product Is Great for a Certain Type of Person.** *Does anyone here have sensitive skin? Or does anyone here suffer from food allergies? Or does anyone here crave sweets? (Change this up to fit your product and solution and share why this product is great for that issue.)*

- **Reason 2: Speak About How Your Company Creates Their Products Differently/Safer Than Other Companies.** *We're one of the only companies that manufactures their products _____! What that means for* *you is that you get safe, premium-grade products for a fraction of the price because we cut out the middle man!*

- **Reason 3: Speak About What Your Company Does for the Environment.** *We are also a green company for these reasons ...*

- **Reason 4: Speak About How Your Company Protects Animals, Children, Etc.** *Raise your hand if you like animals? Good. What we do differently for the safety of animals is this _____.*

- **Reason 5: Speak About Your Company's Founder, Mission, or Charities.** *When you use our products, you are supporting _____ and _____. We have donated over _____ to these two causes with your help through our charitable foundation! And our company was founded in _____ by _____ who had a mission to _____.*

- **Reason 6: Why Your Company Is the BEST** *(Without Bashing Competition). And if you didn't know, out of all the companies that sell _____, we are the number one company in this category in this area.*

Sales 101 Basics

For your presentation, you want to not overwhelm them with every product in your catalog. We show about eight products at our appointment.

That leaves another 150 products we can show at future appointments. It also keeps our presentation to a short 30 minutes plus 15 more for games and a table close.

Do not overwhelm people with a two-hour presentation. It's unnecessary and they might just think you are annoying.

One time, I attended a party and this rep showed us every single product in the catalog. The presentation had a half-time break for food because it was two-and-a-half hours long. We were all suffering a slow death watching her go on and on. By the time it came time to order, people were so fed up, they quickly bought an item and left the party irritated. Don't be that rep.

Features & Benefits

While doing your presentation, speak in terms of features and benefits: The feature is _____ and by using _____, the benefit to you is _____. The hidden benefit to you is _____. And, if you can finish it up with a personal story, even MORE powerful.

- Example:

    ○ Feature: This is a moisturizer and it hydrates for 24 hours.

    ○ Benefit: It gives you more radiant and youthful skin.

    ○ Hidden Benefit: So you get compliments daily from co-workers asking what you are doing differently to look so good.

    ○ My Personal Story: Since I've been using this, my co-workers have been asking me where I've been getting my fillers done because they think

I've been getting fillers! But I don't! That's how amazing this moisturizer is. Infinitely cheaper than fillers and less painful for sure.

- Example:

  o Feature: This pan has a diamond-infused undercoating.

  o Benefit: It makes cooking so much faster.

  o Hidden Benefit: So you have extra time to spend cuddling your kids on the couch every evening because dinner is done in a flash.

  o My Personal Story: One night my mom was coming over and I had nothing ready. I had 30 minutes to make a miracle happen. I was able to throw a frozen steak in this pan and literally by the time she arrived, it was fully cooked with a crisp coating. She was so impressed. This pan is fast and magical, even for frozen food.

Ask Questions to Your Audience During Your Presentation

This will do three things:

1. Help them to decide if your product is a good fit for them.

2. Help you know what their hot-buttons are.

3. Get them to talk about the benefits so they sell themselves.

Step Five: Audience Participation Portion and Presentation

Okay, now we are going to get started with our presentation. Who's excited?! Raise your hand!

This is where you will now walk them through your products. In your presentation, you'll want to focus on asking questions so it's more interactive for your audience.

Focus on features, benefits, and hidden benefits. Plus an occasional story.

If you are new or nervous (like me), I recommend writing up a guide you can follow for your first parties. I used a guide for the first six months until I memorized my presentation. That was my lifeline when I got nervous.

My guide told me which products to use in numerical order and listed out the features, benefits, and hidden benefits with bullet points that I could easily glance at.

If I was tired or forgetful that day, that little guide kept me looking like I was actually smart. I recommend you create your own simple reference guide so you can always look smart on those days when you may be feeling tired or not as quick on your toes. We all have those days. And the show must go on.

On my simple reference guide, I also put one question that I could ask for each product to keep my audience more engaged.

Some good questions to have in your tool belt to ask your audience:

- **The Hot-Button Question**: *When it comes to using [product for your issue] what have been some of the challenges you have faced?*

- **The Struggle Question**: *Anyone struggle with __ or __? This is your miracle right here!*

  - *It gives [this benefit to you] so you get [this hidden benefit].*

- **The Bad Result Question**: *Does anyone know the number one reason a person gets [insert bad result]?*

  - *It's [this reason]. And here's the product that will fix it. And here's why. And here's the [benefit to you] and [the hidden benefit to you].*

- **The Slam Dunk Question**: *Has anyone ever heard of __ before?*

  - *This is our upgraded version of that product. And here's why it's better ...*

- **The Teacher Question**: *Quiz time—What product should you NEVER use on your ___?*

  - *Yes! That product is not intended for that use, but everyone uses it because they don't know better. So, I want to educate you on the proper way to do this ...*

- **The Save Money Question:** *Does anyone know what you will pay for this product at the mall?*

  ○ *Yes, you are right. It's tons more. This product has similar ingredients to those that you would receive at the mall, but you'll only pay a fraction of the price.*

- **The Results Question:** *So how do you like the results so far? What are some words that describe what you are noticing?*

  ○ *Exactly, this is hands down the most powerful ____ on the market and it's chock-full of innovative, clinically proven ingredients that get you results immediately.*

- **The Solution Question:** *Do you know the number one reason that you [bad thing that happens to the person]?*

  ○ *It's ___. So this magic ___ will take away that issue! It also has a powerful [whatever], so you'll get this [added benefit] and this [hidden benefit].*

  ○ *And the best part, it's guaranteed! It's clinically proven to give you results in just ___ weeks of use!*

Step Six: Your Product Presentation Ends | It's Compliment Time

Now, you've finished showing your eight products (or so). If you have a product that gives people noticeable results, have everyone go around the room and compliment one another.

Say this: "You all look FABULOUS! Wow! Compliment time. While I clean up, look around the room and give the person next to you an honest compliment. I'll turn up some music."

That's the sales presentation that I teach to my new rep. Once she has seen it, the next time she can be in charge of a portion of it and lead the show.

Next up, I'll share how we play some games at the party so we never, ever run out of leads.

Chapter 9 | Key Lessons

- **One out of 10 will be your hotshot.** Not everyone. One out of 10. Keep building, keep selling, keep working. Because in all honesty, if you just focus on your personal sales, you can make a fantastic living.

- **Stop thinking you need to have a huge team to finally make money.** Figure out how to make money with your own sales, and then build a team from there. It will feel more authentic when you share with them how much you were able to make selling.

- **Don't drag people along.** Give them the option to join you at your appointments, but slow down for no one. You have no time for small-minded thinking or people who ignore you continuously.

You are a woman on a mission, building an empire.

- **Be prepared for your party.** Cheat sheets and reference guides make you look like a professional who cares about doing well. Stumbling through a presentation with no resource guide makes you look like an amateur. You don't have to know it all, but you do have to be prepared.

- **Go out of your way to build friendships at each appointment.** People are there to have fun, learn new things, make new friends, and go home with great new products. So, make it light, fun, and enjoyable.

- **Don't fill every silence with more information.** Sometimes, less is more. One of my top-selling parties—I actually sold the most out of any party I ever had—they bought because I recognized they didn't want me to talk the whole time. So, I gave them one sentence about each product, and they continued to carry on talking and gossiping as friends. They just had a fun time interacting with their friends, and they thanked me with high sales.

Chapter Ten

Want a Fast and Fun Way to Grow Your Business? Play Games!

The next step in your party is playing two games! These two games are designed to get you more new referrals and more new booked appointments. And the best part? I've tested them over and over again to be sure they actually work.

I've already shared the Fabulous Game, but I'll give you another quick run-through of this game as a refresher:

The Fabulous Game

Hand out the Fabulous Game sheets to everyone, then say:

> *Okay for this next game, is anyone here competitive?*

Point to the ones who raise their hands and say:

> *Okay, that's your fierce competition.*
>
> *We have a prize on the line. You get to pick a gift from the basket in the center of the table.*
>
> *One of you gets to take a gift home from that basket.*
>
> *Like I said in the beginning, I need to see 100 new clients per month to get my new car, so I need your help.*

This is your chance to give your friends the gift of [session name]! If you have anyone in your life who is FABULOUS and deserves a little session like this, you'll put their name and number on the sheet.

Circle "text" if we should text them and "call" if we should call them.

There is a point system: Women over 25 count for three points and women 18 to 24 count for one point. They have to be 18 and older.

Whoever has the most points at the end is crowned our winner and gets a prize from the prize basket. And you can use your cell phones. That's not cheating.

We're going to give you five minutes to play while we clean up around you! All right. On your mark. Get set. GO!!!

Five minutes pass.

Okay, everyone add up your points. Again, three points if they are 25 and older, and one point if they are 18 to 24.

And our winner is Sally!! Everyone let's hear it for Sally! Here's your gift Sally. Here is your crown to wear while you are here.

So for those of you who did not win, and you feel sadness in your heart, don't worry, there is another chance to win!

Deal or No Deal

In my first few months, I didn't play this game because I didn't know about it.

But I was at a company event and a lady who was a top seller was sitting next to me at lunch.

So, I leaned over and asked her what her secret was to get more parties from her current clients.

And she said this, "Deal or No Deal. Google it."

I Googled it, and it was genius.

Sometimes the simplest advice is the best.

I figured it out, put my spin on it, and instantly this game started to book tons more parties for me.

The purpose of this game is to get your audience to say "Deal" and book a future appointment with you to come back with her friends.

Say this:

> *Okay, for those of you who didn't win, I have passed out these little Deal or No Deal envelopes! Don't open them yet! That's cheating!*
>
> *Anyone ever watched the show Deal or No Deal on TV?*
>
> *This is our version of the game! So the way that the game works is: I'm Howie Mandel, except, I have hair! And you'll get the opportunity to say "Deal" or "No Deal" at the end, so here are the rules ...*

There are the three types of parties that you can come back for and they are FREE to attend unless, of course, you decide to make a purchase. I've handed out a cute, laminated card [I designed this in Canva.com] that shows the various parties you can pick from.

The first party is a [Unique Party Title].

At this, we teach you how to …

The second party is a [Unique Party Title].

At this, we teach you how to …

The third party is a [Unique Party Title].

At this, we teach you how to …

Now, the way the game works is this …

You say DEAL if you want to come back, you want to pick a party, you want to invite friends, and you want to win the prize on your Deal Card.

And you say NO DEAL if you don't want to come back, you don't want to pick a party, and YOU HATE winning prizes. [They always giggle here.]

For those of you who said DEAL, just write your prize at the top of your customer card and also write the party you are interested in.

We will set the date when I sit with you one-on-one!

Now, I always give them the gift when they come back for their follow-up appointment. That ensures they will actually come.

Does every DEAL hold? NO, of course not. Maybe 50% hold, but the more you follow up and remind, then it actually will hold.

I need to share this with you.

The first time I ever played this Deal or No Deal Game, it was with five women who were all super sharp and in their early 50s. They all had great jobs and they were the typical crowd that never booked a follow-up party with me.

So I present the game in this new "fun" format and would you believe, of the five women, four say DEAL and three of them actually book parties to come back and bring their friends?!

My mind is blown. I've found yet another way to get more new clients, and it works! From that day forward, I play this at all my parties.

Chapter 10 | Key Lessons

- **Getting referrals will make your life easier.** Find a game, like the Fabulous Game, and play it at every appointment. Organize all your leads in a binder and always follow-up several times to get them booked. Use a variety of different colors and symbols to remind yourself where you left off with each referral. If you prefer to keep track of your leads online or using an app, this is the best program I have found to do that (and it's free): TrackYourContacts.com.

- **Deal or No Deal is effective and fun.** Sometimes just presenting the option to book a party doesn't work. But when you play it as a fun game, people are super into it. Get creative. Creativity sells.

- **Games aren't cheesy.** If you think games are not worth it, play them with a variety of people first. Make your sample size at least 200. Then decide. Games hugely changed my business. Games are not cheesy if you present them in a cool way. Keep it cool.

Chapter Eleven

How a Bad Unicorn Story
Turned into Absolute Magic

*I*n my first few months, typically at the end of my party, I would just give them the option to buy by looking at a sheet with a variety of sets on it, plus some deals. I'd ask them to circle the items they wanted to get started with and put a star on the items they wanted to add to their wish list.

Then I would sit with them one-on-one and take their order.

To recruit, I would follow up to meet for coffee.

But, over the years of studying and learning, I learned an even better system. Even though I'm still sharing my story of how I grew this, I will share this closing strategy that I learned in later years because it's super valuable, and I want you to have the best system.

This system helped me to recruit new reps on the spot, so I am going to share that strategy with you so you get the BEST results.

I read a book called *Rock Your Network Marketing Business* by Sarah Robbins (I'll share more about the full story in two more chapters). It's truly an excellent book from one of the top network marketers in the world. It changed my business almost instantly.

In the book, she shares this …

If your goal is to recruit a ton, then at every party, offer this at your closing for your party:

Option 1: Join My Team

Option 2: Take Home Products

Option 1: Join My Team

Hand out a laminated, color-inked sheet with all the products on one side and the opportunity to join your company on the other. Also, provide a black dry-erase marker.

Then, at the end of every party, say something like this:

Okay, you have two options.

One is to sign up, join our team, and save money while making money.

Option two is to take home products.

Option 1—this is the best option. For $__, you get everything that is shown on this sheet here! It's an insane value to join.

Honestly, I recommend you join over buying products because you can start earning money and saving money on the products you love.

You get:

- *List all the products they get in their kit.*

- *List all the team tools they get.*

    - *A supportive team that shows you the ropes*

    - *My introvert's guide to building a business and meeting strangers*

    - *Weekly training events online (or in person) you can attend*

- *But more importantly, this lets you dream again and will give you hope to:*

    - *Pay off debt*

    - *Pay off college loans*

    - *Pay for vacations*

    - *Afford shopping sprees*

    - *Pay for bucket list experiences with your family*

    - *Pay for schooling for kids and college educations*

    - *Earn a free car*

    - *Afford to give back and help others*

    - *Allow you to be home and present with your kids*

> ○ *Allow you to feel less stressed about money*
>
> ○ *Give you total freedom and flexibility to set your own schedule*

We have three plans available for you:

- *Friends and Family Plan: Pass out catalogs and save on all your products.*

- *Part-Time Plan: About eight hours of your time per week, share our products on the go.*

- *Full-Time Plan: Hold five parties a week. This is the plan I am on. These women are eventually able to replace their full-time income.*

Either way, the choice is yours, but if you like the products, I recommend joining and trying it out for a year. Best case scenario, you make a ton of money. Worst case scenario, you save a bunch of money on products you love.

Some Good Stories to Share That Recruit People to Your Team

Consumable Product Reps: Before I joined our company, I looked at a lot of direct sales companies to figure out which was best. Lots of them sold goods that weren't consumable. Like measuring cups, for example.

It's pretty rare that you will call your rep after the party and say, "Hey those measuring cups that you sold me, I just ran out. Can I get more?" Because those measuring cups rock, and you'll have them forever.

But the difference with our products is that everything we sell is consumable! See this bottle? It runs out. But people are so addicted to our products that they are back on my website ordering when I'm sleeping, or I'm with my kids, or while I'm on the beach relaxing.

Making Money on the Go: I was shopping with my kids one day, and I looked down at my phone because I got an email that said my client had ordered $200.

I make half of what I sell, so in the middle of a shopping center, I made $100.

I suddenly felt wealthy, so I said, "Kids, we are going to Liquid Planet™, and we are going to buy a peanut butter and jelly smoothie. And we will splurge and get two!"

Drama-Free Sorority: When you join our team, we call ourselves the "Drama-Free Sorority." You get drama-free chicks as friends, which we can all use more of!

Seriously, in college, most of us hung out with the guys because we thought the chicks were crazy. So, if you like non-crazy chicks, that's us. We celebrate the amazing moments in life together and cheer each other up during the tough times.

They say you become like the five people you spend the most time with, so if those five people don't lift you up, you need women who bring happiness into your life.

We Are in an Undersaturated Market: 85% of people in this area have never tried or used our products, so it's a WIDE OPEN MARKET, and we are looking for people to help us spread the word about these amazing products.

Option 2: Take Home Products

At this point, I go over all the product sets, the benefits, and the prices. Then share the special deals I am offering.

I say something like:

> *This is option two if you'd like to just get started with some products as a client.*
>
> *The deals you are seeing on this page are only good while you are here with us today, so take advantage of the huge cost savings.*

This creates a feeling of scarcity and urgency, which makes people take action. That fear of missing out causes people to make the impulse decision to buy from you.

Then you can say something like:

> *For payment, we do take cash, check, debit, credit, and Venmo.*
>
> *And we have this unique plan called the H.U.P. Plan. That's the Husband Unawareness Plan. (This is to be said in a silly voice because it's just a silly joke.) That's a little bit of cash, check, and card, so he will never know. (Then you just giggle here.)*
>
> *When we sit together one-on-one, I'll work with you to hook you up with the best deal and payment plan so you can get what you need.*
>
> *Now you can take your marker and circle the items you'd like to get started with and star the items on your wish list. And when we sit one-on-one, I can answer your questions and customize your program for you.*

The Individual One-On-One Sales Close

I pull each client away from the table and sit with them one-on-one.

Next, I say this: "Okay, who is in a rush and would like to sit with me first?"

Then I give her a compliment about the results she's experienced that I can see.

And then I begin asking these questions:

1. *"Did you have fun?"*

2. *"How does your ___ feel?"*

   NOTE: You are asking about how the product you sell made a change to her—adapt this question depending on what you sell.

3. *"If money were no object, what would you like to get started with?"*

   NOTE: You want to get them to think in terms of sets. If they like [one product], ask them if they also liked the [other complimentary product] that works with that [one product].

   I like to say something like:

   "Product A works synergistically with Product B, and in clinical studies was shown to deliver the results you see here when used together."

4. *"Okay, and being more realistic, what would you like to take home today? I can work with you to get you the best deal here, so we can jot things down and figure it out."*

Then write up her order and take payment.

5. *"And, any interest in making extra money?"*

See if she wants to join on the spot; if not, set a date for coffee. Then, schedule her second party.

6. *"Okay, we just need to set a date for you to come back for your next party.*

Looks like three weeks away, I have an opening on Tuesday at 6 p.m. and one on Saturday at noon. What works best for you?"

And that is how you complete your sale.

Will everyone buy? No.

Will you have parties where you sell a ton? Yes.

Will you have parties where you sell nothing? Yes.

Will you have parties with unique people? Yes.

Will you have parties that aren't fun? Yes.

Will you give up? No.

Just remember, it's all part of the game and the challenge.

Not everything goes perfectly all the time. And when things go ridiculously wrong, you always have a funny story to share with others. Those are the best.

I'll never forget one party I went to, which went like this ...

Sometimes I traveled to people, but most of the time they came to me. But, I remember this one, cold night when it was sleeting. I had a party at an apartment complex 30 minutes away.

I get to this building and the parking lot is dark. Really dark. And I'm scared. Looking back, I should have just gone home, but I was being fearless.

I grabbed all my bags and piled them on my shoulders. Typically, I would take one bag in at a time because I wanted to look professional and dainty, but in this situation, I was thinking, *There is no way I am going to go upstairs to the 5th floor of this building and make another trip down in the dark—in the sleeting rain.*

I'm getting sleeted on. I have no umbrella. The stuff I am carrying is heavy. Like, really insanely uncomfortable.

But I am in it to win it.

I ring the outdoor bell. It takes five minutes to let me in. I suffer a small death standing outside in the sleet carrying 8,000 pounds, but I chalk it up to being part of the job and being a warrior of sorts.

I get in the elevator that smells like urine and laugh because I already know this is a good story. Plus, I look like a drowned rat.

I get to the dingy hallway that hasn't been vacuumed in seven years, and I get to the door. It's pretty dirty. I knock, scared.

The door opens.

I'm greeted by a waft of thick, cigarette smoke.

Now, I had forgotten to tell my hostess that we would need to use a table. As I walk in, I realize that might have been something important I should have shared.

There is no table. But there is a small coffee table in the desolate corner of the smoke-filled apartment. Cigarette butts are everywhere and the room is cloudy.

My dream come true. Sleet. Urine. Cigarettes. No table.

Oh, this is going to be a good story. It just keeps getting worse, but I know that this is creating a story that will be so hysterical to share later with others. I'm excited now. I love a good story.

I chuckle inwardly.

Then, I professionally say that we can use the coffee table and sit on the ground.

To her credit, the hostess is super sweet. I am, too. I never lose professionalism. That's my role.

I truly believe we always need to be kinder than we think is necessary because we never know what kind of battle someone is fighting.

She has one guest at her party who doesn't make eye contact with me. I don't think she talks either. It's awkward.

While I am setting up my products, I hear a knock at the door.

Oh good, another guest. I'm excited to at least have a crowd of three.

Just so you can imagine the scene as she enters, this girl is smoking a cigarette, is completely disheveled, and is angry. Now, I love all types of people, so I greet her happily.

She actually hates me. She doesn't operate by the principle of "be kinder than you think is necessary ..." She operates by the principle that she hates me.

I smile. Because she is bigger than me and can kill me.

I feel scared.

Then, I do a little positive self-talk inwardly, *Dude, I'm a freaking unicorn! I'm sparkling and happy. How can you hate me?*

I don't dare say it out loud. She hates me. And I'm not trying to die tonight.

I start my presentation, and I quickly discover she's what we call a "heckler." Hecklers are bad unicorns. They say mean things throughout your whole party to throw you off your game.

I say, "So, this is the product, and the benefit to you is this, and—"

She cuts me off to say, "My A$$ that product does that. This stuff is garbage. Your company just told you to say this ... haha. This stuff sucks."

So there's that.

I share my next product and it continues. She is relentless.

She's like *really* mean. Again, I'm a unicorn, how is this even happening?

I decide to maybe make this my FASTEST party ever known to man. Plus, I can't breathe because the cigarette smoke is stifling. And she might kill me soon.

My typical 45-minute party becomes a 10-minute overview.

I close the party and sell one lip gloss to the hostess. $13.

Phew. At least that pays for my gas.

Get me out of here.

As I am gathering up my things, I throw some Fabulous Game sheets on the table and say whoever gives me the most names wins a prize. Sure enough, they play.

Even the bad unicorn plays.

I take my sheets and head out the door as I award bad unicorn the winner.

I remain calm, professional, and ultra sweet the whole time.

I get back in the urine elevator, meet some shady cats in the hallway, and spring to my car in the sleet. I lock my doors and buzz out of there.

For the bad unicorn, I decide that I won't use her referrals and I rip them up in the car just so I don't forget and accidentally meet her friends.

I give you permission to do the same. If someone isn't your jam, don't message their friends. It's never good. Promise. I've tried it plenty of times to confirm that for you. Her friends would have been nuts. Like 10 times worse bonkers. I've met plenty over the years.

Now I am driving home. I am covered in sleet and freezing. I'm defeated. My only thought is God.

God, please bless my efforts on this one. I know you are blessing my efforts.

That sweet hostess. I genuinely did like her. So I text her referrals the next day.

One of those referrals is the president of the entire Greek Life at Case Western Reserve College. This is an especially nice college in town.

This amazing president ends up connecting me to the head of every single sorority on campus.

I meet hundreds and hundreds of students over the years from her.

I travel to campus.

And they come to me.

And when their parents are in town, they bring them.

I make thousands and thousands of residual income from all those relationships, reorders, and team members that come from that one referral.

So, in all you do, remember that God blesses your efforts. You just have to give him something to bless.

Also, never forget ... Bad unicorns make you stronger. More importantly, they always make for funny stories.

Chapter 11 | Key Lessons

- **Remember to lead with the opportunity at your appointments** if you want to recruit like a machine at all your parties.

- **Or lead with the products** if you want higher sales at your appointments.

- **Practice Option 1 and Option 2 so you sound like a pro.** I took an entire day to practice how I would present those things so I could look like a pro. I pretended I was an actress getting ready for the movie scene of my life. Give it the time it deserves to perfect it.

- **You will meet bad unicorns in your journey.** They are there for a reason—to make you stronger. They are also there for another reason—you'll have funny stories for days.

- **Your efforts will be blessed.** Efforts cannot be blessed if there was no effort. So give it all you've got.

Chapter Twelve

The Disguise
Mean People Wear

Okay, I've got four months to go.

I can meet strangers, book them, sell to them, get referrals from them, book more parties with them, recruit them, and train them.

Game on.

I just keep doing what I am doing. I invite my new reps to join me at networking events and to bring guests over.

I'm starting to realize that it's not only a people business but also a numbers game.

So I keep working the numbers, and my sales and team continue to grow.

Occasionally, while I am spending three hours each day booking new appointments, I'll meet another bad unicorn.

As you know, bad unicorns are mean.

The text conversations go much like this:

> *Hi Sarah! Your friend Jessica Smith just came in for a ___ session and referred you to receive one! Is it better to text you or call you with the details? Michelle*

Bad Unicorn:

> *WT*&#! Who the *&*@(do you think you are? My husband is a lawyer. I'll sue you for messaging me. It's against the law. You just broke the #&\$^ law. If you EVER message me again ... I'm calling the police.*

Oh. Bad Unicorn.

Bad unicorns are just that. Bad.

You see, you will meet bad unicorns in your journey. It's inevitable.

But, here's the truthful story about bad unicorns that you text.

You see, in every home that you get a message like that, there is a 13-year-old boy who lives there. And that 13-year-old boy is playing video games with his best friends.

And he hears his mom's phone ding.

He picks it up and says to his friend, "Look at this crazy message. Let's mess with her."

And he decides to be a bad unicorn and write back to you.

So, anytime you get a message that sounds psychotic, remember that it's just a 13-year-old boy.

No grown woman would have the audacity to talk to you like that. Just not feasible.

What do you do with this bad unicorn?

Bad unicorns get no attention. No replies. No energy.

Bad unicorns get immediately deleted.

Because ultimately, who has time for bad unicorns?

No one.

Now that my team has grown to 15, I am in qualification to become a leader. To make the qualification in the next three months, I have to build my team to 30. The pressure is on.

If I get a team of 30, I also get a free car.

So, what's my strategy?

It's laid out in the next chapter. (This part is only for the good unicorns.)

Chapter 12 | Key Lesson

- **Mean people are just 13-year-old boys.** If you get a mean text or message from anyone, it's just a 13-year-old who picked up his mom's phone and started messing with you. Yes, every single time. There are a fair amount of 13-year-old boys in the world. Ignore them all.

Chapter Thirteen

Big Accomplishments Deserve Big Celebrations

I decide to continue to take the same actions I did in the first month for the next six months.

Now, I know this sounds crazy that this might work.

But it does.

Over the years, I can't tell you how many times in my journey when someone on my team would get stuck or need help. They would all say the same thing:

"I'm stuck. This isn't working."

I would just ask this simple question:

"Tell me this. When things were working, what were you doing differently?"

Usually, it was that they were doing MORE work then.

Truthfully, it's that simple.

Figure it out. Get your system down. Do it a lot. Take others along with you.

And squish bad unicorns.

Armed with this ridiculously simple strategy, I just keep doing the same things, month after month.

Six months roll around, and …

DRUM ROLL, PLEASE.

By the sixth month, I have built a team of 50. Not just 30 but 50!

I have earned a free car, and it even comes with car insurance.

I am earning a pretty steady $5,000 per month.

Can I get a MIC DROP, please??

This means I don't have to get a real job. EVER.

I am a 29-year-old, self-employed powerhouse with newfound confidence.

Six months prior, I was broke.

And while I'm not making exactly as much as I was making before, I will be.

When we hit a new leadership rank, we hold big events at fancy ballrooms. So we host a BIG celebration for my achievement.

Outside the entrance of the building, we park my new car and put a big bow on it.

We make a BIG DEAL.

I invite my boyfriend and he gives a speech about how proud he is of me. And how he was a bit skeptical.

He also shares how hard I worked. I threw myself into this goal, and I made it happen.

He even puts up a funny PowerPoint® slide that shows how my desk was littered with business cards. He's not wrong. I was obsessed with every lead, referral, and booking that I could get my hands on.

I did it. CHECK.

I'm a unicorn, and I got a free car, and I don't need a boss ever again. *I need a crown.*

I did it. My mom is even surprised but tells me she knew I could do it.

My friends still don't understand what I've accomplished. They just know I hit some BIG goal I was working on.

And that's totally cool. I am the only one that has to understand it. And I am thrilled.

Next step? Set a new goal immediately.

I calculate what I need to do to get the next level car, and I work on that. Two months later, I earn another free car.

We host another massive celebration. I'm on top of the world.

And then … things stall out.

Chapter 13 | Key Lessons

- **When things were working, what were you doing differently?** When someone on your team is stuck, ask them that simple question. When you start with, "Tell me this, when things were working, what were you doing differently?" you may find that when they were getting results, they were actually just working their business.

- **You will accomplish your big goals and people won't get it.** That doesn't matter. You get it, and you are who matters most. Not everyone will get it. But your network marketing friends who are big thinkers will get it and cheer you on. Share big news with the big thinkers who understand what you are building.

Chapter Fourteen

What Do You Do When Business Plateaus?

I'm about eight months into my journey.

I'm leading a team of about 70.

I have over 1,000 new clients, some order regularly like Sarah, while others never order again.

I find that for every new client I meet, about one in 20 is a super loyal client like Sarah.

Some just order here and there while others disappear into thin air.

For some reason, my team isn't growing exponentially.

I'm recruiting like a machine, but I'm not raising up leaders. At this point, I can't figure out what I might be doing wrong. A few years later, I do.

Stick with me. I'll reveal the simple fix that changed everything.

My paycheck is a steady $5,000 to $7,000 per month, but I also know there is another level.

Yet, I stay at this level for the next few years.

We go up a bit.

We go down a bit.

We stay even.

But we don't experience massive growth.

Like every good rep learns, I realize the higher the level, the bigger the devil. So, I face challenges.

They come in the form of:

- complaining reps,

- future clients who are canceling appointments,

- new reps who ignore me,

- bad unicorns who yell at me by text,

- customer service issues,

- and on and on.

That's par for the course.

Instead of complaining about it, I realize it's part of the game. No sense in getting worked up over silly, little things that everyone experiences.

I always remind myself, *I will not let one person dictate my success.*

Around this time, I attend a weekend retreat with all my reps at a big hotel in Sandusky, Ohio. It's a two-night motivational event and always a total blast every year we attend.

At this particular event, I have a major mind shift. Major. It was one of those moments that changes everything for me in my life.

One of the top leaders in our company is on stage and she says this:

> *"Ladies, I am here to tell you one very important thing. So listen up. I believe it is our duty to make as much money as possible while we are here on this earth."*

My ears perk up because I'm interested to hear what spin she is going to throw on this.

She continues:

> *"So that you can use that money to be completely debt-free, save tons of money for your future, live below your means, and give back frequently, generously, and anonymously."*

Wow. I've never thought of living like that. I love it. I leave that event on a mission to make more so I can give more. No more playing small.

I decide I need to stop living at the same level and start showing up louder in all areas of life to reach more people.

I remember deciding one night after that event in 2012 that I should start a YouTube channel to serve other network marketers and teach them my introvert success strategies.

I know nothing about YouTube.

I hesitantly load up my first video, and the next morning I wake up to 10 comments in my inbox thanking me for the helpful information.

And I think, "Wow. That's cool. I helped someone. How weird. And how cool. How did they even find it?"

Either way, I don't think much more about it. It makes my heart dance.

I decide that I like to help others, and I like to get their messages, so I start making one video a week and put it on YouTube.

Turns out, it's helpful. It makes me feel fulfilled on the days that I'm handling crying kids, dirty diapers, a messy house, complaining reps, leaders who are frustrated with their business, and canceling appointments.

My YouTube channel is helping lots of people who are thankful for me.

Ultimately, that makes me feel fulfilled.

My YouTube friends keep me afloat emotionally with their sweet comments. While I'm raising a newborn and a three-year-old, it is what I need.

But my channel starts to grow and grow, and it causes eyebrows to raise with the leaders in my company.

They can't understand why I would make videos to help people.

There must be some odd ulterior motive.

There's not, but they can't understand it.

One leader comes to visit and asks me repeatedly why I would make videos and how I am making money from them.

At this point, I'm not making money from them. I don't even know how to do that. But she seems suspicious.

Next month, my phone rings.

I field a call from a top leader who recommends that maybe I stop making videos. She thinks that maybe those videos are pulling me away from actually working my business and maybe it's just not a good idea.

She gets me thinking that maybe she is right. After all, she is a top leader.

So, I ignore YouTube for a month and focus on in-person strategies only.

But I miss it. I love helping people. I love hearing their positive comments. I love making videos. It's my thing. I really love it, and I know it's changing lives.

I start making them again. One per week.

My team continues to grow from my in-person appointments. And, my team has adopted Sarah Robbins' system, so we are growing exponentially.

But, what I didn't anticipate is what happens next.

About six months after posting that first video, I get a text from someone who finds me on YouTube.

She says that she likes my style, and she wonders if she could join my team.

ME?? What??

At first, I thought this can only be a scam. People online are scammers. Someone who finds you on YouTube is obviously a weirdo. Right?

But, I decide to call this person back. Partially out of curiosity. Partially because I'm hoping she is legit. Fingers crossed.

Turns out, she is a real person. She's awesome, and she wants to join my team.

She's been studying how I do things, like the Fabulous Game, and networking events, and she believes she can do the same.

We talk alike, think alike, and have similar stories. It's weirdly amazing.

She was in the industry five years ago and wants to join a new company.

She joins. And she starts working her business from a distance. My mind is blown.

And she's GOOD. She is, like, really doing this. She's motivated. She's excited. And, I didn't even have to recruit her. She found me.

Maybe there is something to this YouTube thing I am doing. Or maybe that was just a fluke.

So, I continue to make one video every week and put it online at YouTube.com/DirectSalesMichelle. The channel still exists to this day, and I am always uploading new videos.

The next month, someone else texts me. Sure enough, she joins my team.

I'm thinking, *Is this real life?*

Initially, I average one to two new reps each month who randomly find me online for the most part. This eventually grows to 5+ reps per month consistently joining my team from my YouTube channel.

Either way, I continue to hold my in-person parties and stay relatively consistent with posting new YouTube videos for free to help others.

At this point, I don't realize how that simple, weekly action will change my life forever …

Chapter 14 | Key Lessons

- **Make as much money as possible while you are on this earth.** The more you make, the more you can impact the lives of those around you. Step up. Be bold. You never know whose life you can change by being fearless.

- **A YouTube channel is always a good idea.** Create a channel to serve people and help them get a new result. Pick a channel that is centered around a topic you LOVE to talk about all day long.

- **Attraction marketing is smart.** In all your videos, never mention the name of the company you work for. People will be curious and ask you who you work for. This is called attraction marketing, and it's what smart network marketers do.

Chapter Fifteen

How I Accidentally Tripled My Business in One Month

*I*t's the summer of 2013. It's a Tuesday night. I have a handful of reps at my house, while other reps on my team are out hosting their own parties at their homes or at other people's houses.

We've grown so big that we can't all use my basement.

We don't have room for 20 cars outside. We have had situations where people have been driving up for their appointments and driving away because there is no room to park.

My neighbors don't say anything, but I'm sure they are over me hosting parties a few times a week that look like a massive graduation party. It's a bit of a zoo with all the cars and madness. Inevitably, my mailbox gets run into by an attendee at least once a month, and it's $200 every time to fix it.

My husband (yes, I married that boyfriend of mine) is a bit over the mailbox debacle every month.

At this point, I'm tired of doing the same presentation day in and day out, so in a moment of laziness, I ask my team to run the whole presentation that evening, and I just sit back.

They coordinate it all and totally ROCK it. They do a fantastic job.

So much so, I realize I've been a dumb leader the past few years.

I always felt the need to LEAD, LEAD, LEAD, and I just let them do little things.

But, in this moment of laziness, I realize they are super competent to do this and I should let them lead.

Letting them lead gives them more confidence and allows me time to take a break.

Duh.

Leadership 101: When you do for someone what they can do on their own, you take away their self-esteem.

Great. I've been a self-esteem stealer for a good four years.

I use this new "let them lead" strategy that entire summer.

I congratulate them and celebrate their work. I write them notes and text them, telling them how amazing they are at the presentation. I breathe belief into them like Maggie did with me.

I'm super impressed with all they are able to sell and how they recruit at the parties.

And sure enough, by letting my team lead, they start to feel like leaders.

Two months after I change my leadership style, my first top leader emerges from my team. She's been on my team for over four years. She quickly builds a team of 30, then 50, and on and on and earns a free car.

Gosh, had I just let them lead from the first week …

Oh Michelle, you self-esteem stealer.

Now, it's January 2014.

And I am on a quest to find a new way to grow my team because I learned at the retreat that we need to make as much money as possible while we are on this earth so we can give back to others.

One night, while on Facebook, I stumble upon a cute blonde with a book for network marketers. I click it.

Now, I already shared a bit of this strategy in a previous chapter, but I did want to share with you the backstory of how all this went down.

I love to learn from anyone in the industry. There are so many unique ideas out there.

Turns out, the book is written by another successful woman in her 20s in networking marketing, and it's called *ROCK Your Networking Marketing Business* by Sarah Robbins.

She talks about how she was a formerly shy teacher who joined her skincare company as a way to make extra money. And initially, for the first few years, she only shared the products (not the opportunity) with tons of people.

She was a top seller for the company and a total selling machine making money selling, but she wasn't growing beyond just the sales.

And she wasn't building a very large team with residual income using that approach.

One day she decided that instead of leading with the products, she would lead with the opportunity that her company offered.

She would offer the opportunity first, and if they decided not to join her company, they could instead become a customer of hers.

She calls this, "Leading with the Opportunity, Defaulting to the Products."

So option number one is JOIN MY TEAM.

If you decide not to do that, option number two is to BE MY CUSTOMER.

Novel idea, but challenging at first for me to digest.

My fear was that I would recruit a bunch of people who just wanted a discount.

But as I kept reading, her story kept getting better.

She went on to become a 7-figure-a-year earner with this approach.

I decide that I am going to use this approach at all of my appointments in April and if it doesn't net good results, I will just stop. No harm done.

My approach looks like this:

I will share for three minutes at the beginning of my appointment about my story. At the end, I will share three minutes about the company and offer them an agreement on the center of the table to join.

After that, I will go over my product sheet. They can make a purchase if they so choose.

When I share my story at the beginning, I decide to change it up from my small story and make it more inspiring.

As your story changes, your story needs to evolve. Delivering a mediocre message serves no one.

I make sure my story is three minutes and ultra impressive.

My goal is to inspire the room. When women are inspired, they want to be a part of what you are growing.

I channel my inner top leader and decide to talk like a leader and share about how this opportunity changed my life, the lifestyle I live now, and why every woman should be a part of this company.

Here is my NEW and IMPROVED introduction:

> *Hi, everyone! Super great to have you all here today. Let's do introductions. Tell us who you are, what you do for work, and something crazy about you, or something you are super excited about.*

> *And now we will tell you about us, who we are, what we do besides this, and why we are obsessed with our company.*

[NOTE: A lot of times I have two or three reps with me at appointments. I always go last. I let them lead now because I'm not being a self-esteem stealer anymore.]

> *So, my name is Michelle, and I joined this company at 23*

years old, after graduating college while working as a pharmaceutical sales rep.

I had a great job and attended a company event. There was a lady in the room who just earned a free car, another that made 6-figures, and another who was a millionaire, and I just thought ... And these ladies don't have bosses?

It sounded so amazing, so I ended up joining at 23—even though my mom told me it may not work out.

For the next six years, I got a major discount on all my products, but I didn't do much with my business. It was just my backup plan in case I lost my job. Which I will tell you, every woman today should have a backup plan in today's tumultuous economy.

So for six years, I had about five customers because I was too shy to tell anyone I sold, but it was nice knowing I had a backup plan.

Then at age 29, I lost my corporate job and without a job or money coming in, I decided to give this a try for six months because I kept thinking of those ladies with free cars making 6-figures.

So, I was going to try for six months, and when it didn't work, I was going to quit.

As luck would have it, there was a lady who lives two miles from here who has been a top earner, driven 11 free luxury cars, earned over $2 million in her career, and she said she would mentor me.

What I loved about this woman was that she was super

humble, and she actually has a social anxiety disorder, gets nervous talking in front of people, and she fainted at her first party ... So she gave me hope—hope that I didn't have to be a perfect, loud, pushy, abrasive lady to be successful at this.

After following her simple system of using text messaging to meet people, the first month I made $1,000, which got me thinking that if I could just double or triple that, this could be a legitimate source of income for me.

Now, I don't need a lot in life. I grew up in a broken family, incredibly poor. We couldn't afford the things we wanted. Some years, we even got Christmas gifts from people in our community. So, I come from very humble beginnings.

Fast forward, six months later. I kept following her system, and I earned my first free car, earned over $5,000 that month, and I said, "Game On!" I thought, This is what I will do forever! Five thousand dollars was a ton of money for me!

So, that was five years ago for me, and in the last five years, I have been boss-free. And financially free.

I was able to pay off over $15,000 in credit card debt and $20,000 in college loans.

I now live totally debt-free, have tons of savings for my future, and I am able to give back frequently, generously, and anonymously, to local families in need.

That's what drives me every day to get up because I want everyone to know about this amazing company and what it can do for your life. So after your appointment, I'll be sharing more about the company if you or someone you know is looking for extra money or a change.

So let's go ahead and get started with the products.

And at the end of the appointment, I would revisit what I said and I'd say again, "Like I mentioned at the beginning, here is the option to join our happy family."

I'd go over the details of the kit to join.

I'd talk about the residual income of reorders and how a business can produce income for you even when you aren't working.

I'd tell them how it's the most amazing retirement plan in the world.

I'd go over the training, the friends, the support, etc.

After I cover about three minutes of those details, I set a pile of agreements in the center of the table for anyone who wants to sign up.

Then, whether or not they decide to sign up, I go over the products we used. I say something like, "Now let's go over the products we used." Then I introduce the sheet that has the product sets they can purchase.

So, let's go back to April, after I had just finished reading the book.

Here's how it played out when I changed about six minutes of my appointment.

The results were astounding.

My doorbell rang for my appointment. I had two clients that day. I was nervous to use my new approach but decided to try out my new system on her.

And would you believe at the end, she said, "Okay, great. Yes, I'll join your team, and I'd also like to take home these products I circled for my daughter."

So I basically fell over dead. What just happened?!

I kept my composure and said, "Great!" And I pulled out an order form and wrote up her order. I totaled it up, and while I ran up to get her items, I gave her the agreement to fill out.

Now, I was nervous. I was wondering if she was really joining or was she just confused, or what. I couldn't believe it.

And would you believe she went home, told her husband all about this inspirational story of this woman (ME!), and her husband was all 100% on board? WHAT?!

They watched the new rep orientation video together, and the next week she ordered a big inventory store and got started.

I am literally dying with excitement.

Was it really this easy?

She didn't just want a discount because she was inspired by my story.

INSPIRED.

Inspired people take action.

It made me realize that it is SO important that we have super inspirational stories. When someone *joins inspired* and with a dream in their heart, they will do much more with this opportunity.

They won't just do the minimum.

Appointment two arrived at my door that day, one hour later.

She brought her husband. Same conversation, same everything. And her husband said, "Wow, sounds great!" And she signed up, too.

Two women signed up that day. I continued this for the rest of the month and signed up 22 recruits personally. My unit caught wind of it, and they also recruited about 20 additional team members.

What I found about these women was that after they joined and watched their welcome video, they were even more excited about the possibilities of what this could do for their lives.

It was almost like I just needed to bring people in, expose them to our world, and let them decide what to do with it.

Some of them, who I literally just thought were joining to sell to a few friends, went on to become top reps in our unit. And of course, some did absolutely nothing.

But either way, lives were being changed because they were inspired. Inspired women do not join for a discount only.

THEN, this amazing thing happens.

I get an email.

It's someone new who finds me on YouTube. Turns out, over the years, she's been messaging me and I've been responding and helping her by answering her questions here and there. I didn't think much of my actions other than, I just like helping people.

Well, those little interactions secured in her heart that I am the person she wants to join with. She loves my style and my training. And she claims she will be a total rockstar and will shoot to the top of the company very quickly.

She joins. Would you believe … this girl Stephanie recruits 20 people in her first month and becomes a top 1% leader in the second month and basically skyrockets to the top of her business, bringing in over 700 people to her team … adding over 700 people to my downline?!

MIND BLOWN.

She found me on YOUTUBE of all places.

And she *still* is today one of my best friends ever. All because I decided to hit the record button.

Another phone call. A girl from Tennessee named Sierra, who is a mom to a little one. She's been following me for years. She wants to be a top leader and wants to join my company. And she does. And she also shoots to the top of the company as a top 1% leader.

And today *she is still* one of my best friends ever. Again, all because this introvert decided to hit record on YouTube.

So pile all this awesomeness together and in April, my team sales went from pretty steady to suddenly tripling and quadrupling. My commission skyrockets to $17,963 that month.

And this is funny, in the middle of August, I hopped on my company website to look at my car report to track how close I am to earning the company luxury car.

It shows the dollar amount I need to sell to get the luxury car. Well, I was so used to seeing over $36,000 more needed to sell to hit the goal, I had basically stopped looking at that report.

When I logged in, the number needed to finish the luxury car was $0.

Again, I fell over dead.

We finished the luxury car one and a half months early.

I don't tell you any of this to impress you, but to impress upon you that this all changed because of three things:

1. My mission changed to make more money to help more people. Because of that, I started to act and lead differently.

2. I changed the format of my appointments.

3. I started to hit record and make YouTube videos.

We continued doing this, and in the middle of May, we accidentally qualified for the top leadership trip to London with all the big shots *an entire month and a half early.*

Chapter 15 | Key Lessons

- **Be open to trying new strategies and systems from a variety of experts.** Don't just follow people in your company. Sarah Robbins is a top network marketer in the industry, and by picking up her book, I learned unique and different strategies not being taught at my company. Follow people from lots of companies to find the best strategy that can change everything for you. There are lots of very smart people within your company and within other companies. Don't limit your learning.

- **Do it afraid.** You might feel like you can't change your story to be inspirational, or you can't film a YouTube video, but in all honesty, yes you can. Change your thinking and go for it. It could change your life forever. Do it anyway, girl.

Chapter Sixteen

What It Looks Like to Work Smarter, Not Harder

At this point, my YouTube channel is starting to really grow, and some people in my company think I am up to no good having a YouTube channel. It makes me sad because I don't agree.

Because I know it's ONLY good.

It's bringing in new reps.

It's bringing in more revenue for the company (like millions of dollars).

I am changing lives.

And I'm doing everything to comply with company rules.

It is what the very smart and strategic network marketers do. They build brands and they are the center of the brand.

I study this. I know this.

I realize the power of attraction marketing. That is the simple act of attracting more business to you by the free training you offer to others.

I know that it's important to brand myself.

It's called BRANDING 101 for network marketers.

Brand yourself. Not your company.

When you brand you, you will organically attract a tribe online.

Conversely, when you brand your network marketing company, you will attract only people in your company.

I'll share more about this in my next book: *You Are a Million Dollar Brand.*

Then, I get a message on Facebook.

"Michelle! You were just on *The Today Show.*"

What?? *The Today Show* picked up one of my YouTube videos and featured a clip on their show. I didn't even know. I can't believe it.

And then, I get an email.

I get a call from a CEO of a direct sales company, and they ask to fly me out to come speak and train their reps. Because they like my style on YouTube.

MIND. BLOWN.

The six-year failure is now getting asked to speak. I can't believe this.

Of course, I say yes. They even pay me a lot of money.

They tell me to bring my training program. I don't have one. I don't have much time before the event, so I make one that night.

I head into my son's room with my computer. It's the only quiet room in the house.

I grab a headset and start recording my training on how to generate leads, team build, and hold a party.

Then, I Google "How to make a CD."

I get it burned onto a CD, and I get artwork done.

I bring my new CDs to my speaking engagement in Utah. I sell tons.

Then, I mention it on my YouTube channel and everyone wants copies.

I start shipping them all over the world. Yes, the WORLD!

It's reaching reps from all different types of companies.

Again, MIND BLOWN.

Then, I put it on a website: DirectSalesRocks.com.

I sell tens of thousands.

I can't believe it. Then, I start to realize I'm helping people more and more as email messages flood in.

I love it. I love hearing success story after success story of people who decided to step up and make things happen.

Because I understand their pain of being stuck.

I know it so well, it hurts. It still hurts to think about those days. I was utterly exhausted with my thoughts and dreams that developed into nothing for six years.

It's almost surreal that the broken, shy girl from humble beginnings can actually help anyone else, but I don't question it because people keep saying thanks.

My heart dances every day I read those messages.

I keep serving up new videos because this mission seems bigger than me. I feel like I've been called to help others who have been stuck like me.

Then, I make one key discovery and everything explodes ...

Chapter 16 | Key Lessons

- **You reap what you sow.** Put yourself out there. Be louder, prouder, bolder, and in charge. Amazing doors will open for you and opportunities will start to come your way that you never dreamed possible.

- **Video is a game changer.** If you want to start spreading your message far and wide and impacting the world, make videos to help people. I mean it. Even if you have only sold $300 at one party. There is someone out there that has never sold $300 at a party and needs you to inspire them into action. You are an expert in the eyes of someone when you teach them something they haven't learned before. Let that sink in. Therefore, you are an expert. And if you don't know how to make videos, I have a free training where I show you how here:

  VideoCreatorClassroom.com/Register

- **You don't have to be the biggest and the best to start showing up bolder online.** You just have to decide to go for it and serve others. It's not about you. It's about whose life you can impact today. And some of the biggest and best just haven't done it, so there is room for you.

Chapter Seventeen

The One Thing
That Shifted Everything

I'm on Facebook and I stumble upon this dude, who is apparently a super successful network marketer. I start to study his trainings, and I learn that he was the #1 income earner for his network marketing company.

He's poised, confident, well-spoken, and smart. And he has been using Facebook Live to attract success online. It's intriguing to me.

His name is Ray Higdon. His wife Jessica is also ridiculously smart about marketing on Facebook. I continue to follow them because I like their style. It's direct, bite-sized, and actionable.

And then I notice they have a Facebook Live challenge called the 14-Day Challenge. I buy the course and take this challenge to go live for 14 days in a row. Honestly, the idea of it is horrifying, but it forces me into action.

I go live for 14 days in a row, somewhat clueless about what I am doing, but it gives me confidence to start going LIVE on Facebook consistently.

It's December 2018. I get a call from one of my top leaders in Tennessee. It's Sierra. She is one of those people who found me on YouTube a few years prior. She's a go-getter. She also has a dry sense of humor that's super fun, so I love when she calls.

She has been trying out some new strategies and has some good news to share.

My team and I are always thinking outside the box.

Always pushing the envelope.

Always innovating.

She loves this stuff.

"What? This sounds good. What is it?" I'm dying.

She says, "Okay, so I just recruited someone who lives in Texas. Like, on the computer. And I sold her some products, too."

"Wait, what? That's insane. How?" I ask.

She says, "Well, I mailed her some samples, and then I video-chatted with her and I did a party just like we do them in-person. And she joined my team and bought products from me."

My mind races. I congratulate her. I hang up the phone.

It's genius.

Brilliant.

I can't sleep over it. I keep thinking about how we could do this on a larger scale.

I keep thinking, *Couldn't we just host one very large party online and send everyone samples, and then have everyone watch at the same time?*

I believe it will work.

I stay up late that night and type up a plan of action.

We will hold one massive Facebook Live event. At this point, I'm now confident on Facebook Live, which is a skill I had to master.

I'll invite my entire team, and they can invite all their clients.

I make a checklist for my team with all the product samples we will send.

Then, I pick a date and time we will hold the event.

I finalize it all by making an event guide for our guests that walks them through all the products in case they join the Live late.

The next day, I tell my team that I have a very special idea planned for three weeks away. An online Facebook Live event.

Some of them are on board. Others think I'm nuts.

I am nuts. That's already been confirmed.

Either way, the ones who are on board invite guests and mail them samples.

The date comes. I'm nervous. What the heck am I doing? I don't even know if this will work.

Whatever. Too late now for that kind of thinking. *Figure it out, Michelle.*

So, I go live just like my friend did. And I walk my audience through how to use the products. Except, instead of it being an audience of one, mine happens to be an audience of 450.

What have I done? 450 humans?! Oh my word.

I better not screw this up. My whole team is counting on me. And all their clients are watching.

I tell my two- and five-year-old kids to not bother Mommy for 45 minutes while I am in my office, and my husband keeps them occupied.

It's game time. I have the party of a lifetime.

I get started, and I realize this is infinitely easier than an in-person party because:

1. No one can interrupt me.

2. No one can heckle my party.

3. I'm saying the same thing I say every day at my actual party.

4. I don't have to leave my house, pack my car, or hire a babysitter.

I finish the 45-minute Live.

Sales roll in over the next 7 days. Over $20,000 in team sales. Over 20 new recruits. All because of a 45-minute Live.

I'm elated. Is this real life? The most I've ever sold at an in-person party has been $1,400. And the most I have ever recruited at one party is five people. This is INSANE.

Word spreads quickly about our very profitable Facebook Live and my inbox explodes with questions. I get so many messages that I struggle to reply to them all.

So, I put together a free training to share this with anyone in the industry who wants to know how to host Facebook Live parties online sharing our success tips.

You can grab it here:

MasteringTheLive.com/FreeTraining

I hear from so many that the training radically changes their business.

I continue to host these events every three weeks with my team. I find that some team members like to participate who had otherwise been doing nothing, because it's a new spin and it's easy for them to invite guests.

And it's fun to switch things up.

So at this point, I know how to:

- Meet strangers

- Book them for appointments

- Sell to them

- Get referrals

- Book future parties with them

- Recruit them

- Deal with bad unicorns

- Use YouTube to attract business

- Use Facebook Live to crush sales and recruit like a machine

I'm learning.

And I now have seen the true power of social media.

Wow. Social media works to sell products and recruit. Clearly.

Chapter 17 | Key Lessons

- **Facebook Live is a skill you need to master.** If you can host a party in front of an audience, you can host a Facebook Live. It's easier and just about the same as an in-person party. And you can hold it in a private group with only the people you want to see it.

- **Social media has the potential to exponentially grow your business.** Use it wisely, but not all the time. Don't give up on what you are doing that is working, just add this in, master it, and make decisions on your plan of action from there.

- **Don't believe that social media will suddenly change everything tomorrow.** It takes time, so continue to do what works while learning the various platforms.

Chapter Eighteen

Top 11 Takeaways
from an 18-Year Adventure

I could go on and on and write this book forever because I have so many unshared stories and chapters I would add.

But, I couldn't stop writing until I tell you these 11 VERY IMPORTANT THINGS:

1. **YOU have the internal power to get out of your own way.** Change your thinking and do something radical like leave a job that doesn't serve you and step it up. When you treat your network marketing business like your REAL JOB, real things start to happen real quick. Give yourself no other option. No matter what holds you back, do it anyway, girl.

2. **None of this will be easy, but it will be worth it.** Get back up, brush yourself off, and remind yourself you are an amazing unicorn. Because you are made for more.

3. **One step at a time, you will build your business.** It doesn't happen overnight. So don't think you will be an overnight success. You will be a success when you are committed daily to your success. Consistency wins every time.

4. **Get ready for the roller-coaster ride of your life.** Some days will be stellar. Others will be terrible. It's ups and downs all the time for the rest of your career. It's a roller coaster, so hang on and keep the dream within sight. People will buy from you, then return things. They will confirm their appointment five minutes before and forget to show up. They will book coffee appointments with you, and then not show up while you sit in the coffee shop. They will join your team and then ignore your calls forever. They will join your team and shoot to the top of leadership, and then quit. I have a story for EVERY scenario ... and when you are going through it, just send me a message on Facebook and I'll reply, "Oh, that's normal." Because it is. So just stay the course. Let's connect:

Facebook.com/DirectSalesMichelle

5. **Your success in the industry can take you to places you never dreamed of.** Work it and give it all you've got because you will be paving a path for yourself that is exponentially more than you ever imagined.

6. **If you work for two network marketing companies your energy will be split 50% between both.** What's a 50% in school? An F. What's 100% in school? An A+.

7. **The higher the level, the bigger the devil.** People will be mean sometimes. Clients, Leads, Reps, Leaders. Those confrontations will make you stronger. I know this because I've faced them all and they gave me confidence to know I can handle anything. Welcome

the difficulties. You need those moments to be able to walk your teammates through how to handle it when it happens to them. And remind yourself, *I am just a unicorn doing the best I can spreading joy and love throughout the world.* Not everyone will love your style and that's okay. You just need to love you. And you are a unicorn, so you're perfectly lovable.

8. **Quitting is NOT an option.** There will be moments when you feel like quitting. In those moments, pull out your vision board. And, remember that quitting this is NOT an option. I never, ever, ever considered quitting while I was building. I also never ever complained to my spouse, my family, or my friends. They were not in the industry and didn't understand the journey, so I didn't ask them for advice. Take advice from one person you would like to trade places with within the industry. End of story.

9. **God gave you two ears and one mouth for a reason.** People want to be heard. Practice compassion and love. Never holding a grudge. For you are a walking unicorn. A sparkly, loving unicorn.

10. **Stay in your lane.** Pretend you are a train on its own track. The train to the left and right of you do not affect how slow or fast you move. So, why would you look at them or wait for them? That would be silly. Don't compare your journey to anyone else's journey. To compare is to despair. Don't follow people online who make you feel less powerful. Instead, focus on how you can compete with yourself to be the best version of you.

With your blinders on, you will achieve success you never dreamed of.

11. **On your journey to where you are going, never forget where you came from.** Your journey will be part of your story one day, so make sure it isn't perfect. Perfect stories are boring.

Here's the truth:

It's possible for you.

It's possible for you at any point in your journey to stop, think a bigger thought, and start taking action.

No matter what you struggle with, do it anyway.

Things change the day that you make a decision that you will no longer settle for a life that is less than you deserve.

Mediocrity is a disease, and when you choose to rise up and shine, you will inspire a whole tribe of others to be great.

I shared my entire story so you can see how it unfolded because the hardest part of seeing someone's success is not knowing their struggle.

My struggle is real.

My shyness is real.

My introverted self is real.

My self-limiting beliefs are real.

I'm not perfect. I'm not the smartest. I'm not the most techie. I'm just a girl who knows how to use Google, challenge the norm, and study the ways that others market and sell.

Be obsessed with learning.

Be obsessed with innovation.

Be obsessed with pushing the boundaries.

Be obsessed with questioning things that don't seem right.

Finally, I believe that every single obstacle that is thrown your way does one of two things:

1. Makes you stronger and more powerful for having gotten through it.

2. Makes for a really, really funny story you can share later.

Because, let's be honest, bad unicorns make for really great stories.

Chapter Nineteen

You Are Meant for Greatness!

*I*n 2019, my little YouTube channel is averaging 5+ new reps per month to my team.

And, that year, it becomes very clear that God has a different plan for me.

My online brand has grown so big that it's becoming challenging to manage both the brand and my network marketing business. And the brand is bringing in over six times the income.

I also really love creating videos and training programs and teaching others in network marketing all about branding online.

One could say I am obsessed with videos and branding. It's literally all I want to do and talk about.

I know I have to make a tough decision.

I pray about it for a solid year before making any rash decision but decide in October 2019 that I am being called to train on a new platform.

I've grown my team from just me to recruiting thousands over the years, all while being able to work from home, earn an executive income, and raise my kids. I feel called to train others around the world and show them how to build it big.

So, I let go of building my own network marketing business and embark on a journey training others to build their businesses, showing them how to step into their greatness.

And I love it. I love serving others, helping them step into their greatness, seeing them achieve wins they didn't think were possible. My heart dances every time I get a little message like this online:

> "Thank you" is nowhere near enough to say to our beloved Michelle Cunningham. From the time I bought her very first course (on a CD 😆) last year to last night, I have become a Director in my direct sales company, branded myself, have multiple streams of income, and just earned the free use of a 2021 Chevy Malibu!!! What in the world?! 💁 🌍
>
> Buy ALL of her courses! Every.single.one. and follow them exactly. When you do, I'll see you at the top!!! 🦄 🙌 — 😇 feeling blessed.

We are not meant to blend into life.

We are meant to stand out.

When we do, we are giving others permission to do the same.

That online brand quickly hits over 7-figures in revenue in just 18 months, and I realize this is what God has called me to do next.

I consider it an incredible blessing. I absolutely love my online tribe of friends who I appropriately call my unicorn friends.

You, my friend, are a unicorn. I adore you and believe in your greatness. No matter how crazy your ideas are, I support them.

I support your out-of-the-box thinking and your need to push boundaries. And I will cheer you on!

The world needs more of that.

I love being connected with you in our Facebook community where we all share ideas and support one another.

And if you aren't in the community, it's free to come join us:

DoItAnywayGirl.com/Club

I go live twice a week in my Facebook tribe. We can chat, you can ask questions, and I give away gifts. Because who doesn't LOVE gifts?

Key Lessons from my being afraid and doing it anyway:

- **God has a master plan**. Listen. Pray about it. And follow your heart.

- **The world needs more of you**. Your stepping out into your greatness will not only change your life but it will also inspire others into action.

ACKNOWLEDGMENTS

To my mom, who is my biggest fan, my best friend, and supporter. Thank you for everything you did for us as kids. For never giving up, fighting through the tough times, and creating your dream life. You inspire me daily.

To my husband, Brian, thank you for being my love. And for supporting me while I worked on these weird entrepreneurial goals over the years. I love you, babe.

To my two kids, Brady and Alyssa, who always remind me that the simple things in life really matter. You both will change the world in your own unique ways. You make Mom and Dad so proud. I am so glad God gave me you both. You are the best things that ever happened to me, my little angels.

To my network marketing recruiter Rachada and her husband Sam. Sam, thanks for convincing me to go to that hotel event with your wife. Rachada, thanks for convincing me to join your team. The spark that started it all. And thanks for introducing me to Betsy, our leader who is an incredible inspiration with the sweetest heart.

To Maggie, the mentor that believed in me, challenged me, and changed everything for me. Thank you for believing in me endlessly. And thank you for being one of my best friends and cheerleaders in the world. You have changed my life forever. I adore you.

To my amazing friends who reviewed the book and provided your valuable feedback, helping to shape the book. Stephanie Blake, Ray Higdon, Julie Burke, Kimberly Olson, Maggie Rader, Marina Simone, Sonia Molina, Kelsey Saunders, Tomilyn Garot, Laquesha Thompson, Cindy Strong, Stephanie Machina, Sarah Zolecki, Shamecca Stephens, Stamatia Tsakos, Charyse Williams, Stacey Killam, Sierra Tippens, Adrienne Gummerson, Bridgette Carstens, Kathryn White, Dagmar Torres, Joanna Saunders, Jennifer L. Henrich, Tracy Daebelliehn, Francesca Suarez, Michelle Mahoney, Kathryn Rebernick, Dorothy-Inez Del Tufo, Diana Decker, Kimm Brown, and Noukouchee Xiong. I adore and love you!

Sarah Robbins, one of my idols in the network marketing space, THANK YOU for reading my book and writing the foreword. Over the years, you have grown my business exponentially because of the trainings you've put into the world. Your book, *ROCK Your Network Marketing Business,* changed everything for me. Thank you for all you do to elevate this profession.

To my book editor, the queen of editing, Lori Lynn. Thankful that Dan Henry recommended you. You are the kindest, most caring, and most detailed person I've ever met. I can't believe someone actually enjoys editing, but God has gifted you that insane talent. Thank you for taking my ideas and making them sound superb.

To Justice Eagan, the king of marketing and copywriting. Thank you for helping me craft the perfect name for this book. You are a genius, essentially.

To the best photographer in the world, Shannon Ahlstrand! Thank you for being so fun, so creative, and so amazing to work with. You made this front cover come to life! You are a brilliant and talented photographer.

And to my network marketing team that I've had the privilege of leading. Thank you for being super unique, keeping it real, being hysterically funny, and being fierce. You all have made this the best journey I could have ever been on. It's been hysterical the entire way. Oh, the stories we can tell! You all are crazy. And that's why I love you. The adventures we've had … well, that's another whole book in itself.

ABOUT THE AUTHOR

*M*ichelle Cunningham is on a mission to empower women to rock their direct sales/network marketing business so they can live more freely, give more generously, and be completely present for the ones they love.

During her 17 years in the industry, Michelle was recognized by her network marketing company for being one of the top-sellers and top-recruiters year after year, earning countless diamonds, luxury cars, and exotic trips. She led her power-house team to be one of the top-selling teams in the nation. She was honored with the most prestigious award given by the company for being giving of her thoughts and ideas to others within her organization.

Michelle raised her kids as a work-from-home network marketing mom and was always present with her little ones during the day and never missed any magical moments. She resides in North Carolina with her husband of 10 years, Brian, and two kids, Brady and Alyssa.

Michelle can be found on YouTube creating silly videos that help network marketers at YouTube.com/DirectSalesMichelle.

She also is on Instagram "trying" to post cool things at Instagram.com/DirectSalesMichelle.

She loves going live on Facebook so she can chat with you. You can catch her live every Monday and Wednesday at 1 p.m. EST inside her Facebook group, which you can join here: DoItAnywayGirl.com/Club.

Michelle has several online courses that help network marketers achieve greater success in less time.

Her wildly popular CDs and audio downloads that have sold tens of thousands of copies can be found at DirectSalesRocks.com.

Her online branding training that shows network marketers how to stand out and win on Facebook can be found at 21DayBrandingChallenge.com.

Her Facebook Live™ course that teaches network marketers how to host profitable online parties in 45 minutes flat is available at MasteringTheLive.com.

Her YouTube™ Success Video Creator Classroom Course is available at VideoCreatorClassroom.com.

Her mantra? "Successful women feel the fear and do it anyway."

Find her fun website with many free resources for direct sellers at **MichelleCunningham.com.**

Made in the USA
Las Vegas, NV
23 May 2023

72456556R00115